THE STATE OF THE WORLD'S CHILDREN
1996

Oxford University Press, Walton Street, Oxford, OX2 6DP, Oxfordshire, UK. Oxford, New York, Toronto, Delhi, Bombay, Calcutta, Madras, Karachi, Kuala Lumpur, Singapore, Hong Kong, Tokyo, Nairobi, Dar-es-Salaam, Cape Town, Melbourne, Auckland and associated companies in Berlin and Ibadan.

Oxford is a trade mark of Oxford University Press.
Published in the United States by Oxford University Press, New York.

British Library Cataloguing in Publication Data
The state of the world's children 1996
1. Children—Care and hygiene
613' 0432 RJ101

ISBN 0-19-262747-3
ISSN 0265-718X

The Library of Congress has catalogued this serial publication as follows:
The state of the world's children—Oxford and New York: Oxford University Press
for UNICEF
v.; ill.; 20cm. Annual. Began publication in 1980.
1. Children—Developing countries—Periodicals.
2. Children—Care and hygiene—Developing countries—Periodicals. I. UNICEF.
HQ 792.2. S73 83-647550 362.7' 1'091724

UNICEF, UNICEF House, 3 UN Plaza, New York, NY 10017, USA.

UNICEF, Palais des Nations, CH-1211, Geneva 10, Switzerland.

Cover photo
Greece, circa 1946, ICEF-278

Back cover photo
Mauritania, 1988, UNICEF/C88-17/Goodsmith

THE STATE
OF THE WORLD'S
CHILDREN
1996

Carol Bellamy, Executive Director,
United Nations Children's Fund

Published for UNICEF by
Oxford University Press

Contents

Chapter I
Children in war

Wars and civil conflicts are taking a massive toll on children. The numbers, though imprecise, are devastating: approximately 2 million children have been killed during the last decade, and between 4 million and 5 million disabled. Twelve million more have been uprooted from their homes, and countless others face the heightened risk of disease and malnutrition and of separation from their families.

International law provides standards for protecting children in war. These standards must be vigorously enforced to create a zone of peace for the young. UNICEF, founded to provide emergency relief for children in the aftermath of World War II, takes this opportunity in its 50th anniversary year to set out an Anti-war Agenda, a series of vital, practical actions to help stall the momentum of violence. The Agenda calls for an end to the recruitment and conscription into the military of children under the age of 18, for a ban on the manufacture, use, stockpiling and sale of all anti-personnel land-mines and for strengthening of procedures to monitor and prosecute war crimes. The Agenda also urges support for long-term development, reconciliation, rehabilitation and education for peace.

Chapter II
Fifty years for children

This chapter traces UNICEF's and the world's response to the needs of children, starting with the 1950s, when mass campaigns promised to end a number of infectious diseases, including tuberculosis, yaws, trachoma, leprosy and malaria. The 1960s' focus on eradicating poverty grew during the 1970s into the development of flexible, community-oriented initiatives. Then in the 1980s, with economies in decline, UNICEF launched the 'child survival and development revolution', which, through simple, cost-effective methods, saved more than 12 million children's lives by the end of the decade.

With the 1990s, a new era has opened for children, with the world making great strides towards achieving the World Summit for Children's basic health, nutrition and education goals for the year 2000 and a campaign that has brought universal ratification of the Convention on the Rights of the Child nearly within reach. Looking towards the year 2000 and beyond, children are increasingly at the centre of the international human rights and development agenda, and despite the depredations of war and poverty, global progress is possible.

The material in this chapter draws on the historical research of Maggie Black on UNICEF, including her books *Children First: The story of UNICEF past and present* (UNICEF/Oxford University Press, to be published in 1996) and *The Children and the Nations* (UNICEF, 1986).

Chapter III
Statistical tables

Statistics provide an essential foundation for gauging children's well-being and are vital indicators of the care, nurture and resources that children receive in their communities and countries. We are reminded that more than 12 million children each year continue to die from the 'silent' emergencies of preventable diseases and malnutrition. Statistics such as those on infant and child mortality, immunization, maternal mortality, malnutrition and school enrolment chart the progress countries are making towards the goals set at the World Summit for Children and in overcoming disparities, such as the discrimination against girls and women. Basic indicators on nutrition, health, education, population, economic progress and the situation of women are given. Regional summaries are also provided.

Panels

Text figures

Regional spotlights

"The most important meaning of this Nobel award is the solemn recognition that the welfare of today's children is inseparably linked with the peace of tomorrow's world."

Henry R. Labouisse, Executive Director of UNICEF (1965-1979), in his acceptance of the Nobel Peace Prize in 1965 for UNICEF.

Foreword

It was the suffering of children in war that prompted the founding of UNICEF 50 years ago. It is the continuing suffering of children that reminds us how much more we need to do, and how enormous is the task still before UNICEF. *The State of the World's Children* report this year examines what it calls "the terrible symmetry" framed by these 50 years.

Please join me in supporting the urgent effort to bring peace to children—peace in every sense of the word; building an ethic against violence directed at children, against drafting children as combatants, against planting anti-personnel land-mines and against holding children as hostages. And, as affirmed by the Declaration of the 1990 World Summit for Children and enshrined in the 1989 Convention on the Rights of the Child, may nations abide by the principle of "first call for children" always—with their survival, protection and development given high priority—in times of adversity as well as in times of beneficence, in times of war as well as in times of peace.

UNICEF has worked and has encouraged others during this half-century to make this principle a reality. This report documents that great work. I recommend these pages to all readers. They reflect our common hopes and they summon us to even greater common action on behalf of the children of the world.

Boutros Boutros-Ghali
United Nations Secretary-General

Orphaned children in Baidoa, Somalia.

Preface

This special issue of *The State of the World's Children* marks the 50th anniversary year of UNICEF. As such, it aims to fulfil three purposes. First, it proposes an agenda against war as a vital step to prevent and alleviate the suffering of children in armed conflict. We start with children in war because their contemporary predicament is both overwhelming and inescapable.

Second, it reviews the efforts of UNICEF in its first half-century to cope with children submerged not only in conflict but also in the silent emergencies of poverty and preventable disease. And it shows how many governments and communities, with UNICEF support, have made great progress in improving the health, nutrition and education of their children.

Third, it retains the annual presentation of carefully assembled statistical data, so that the progress towards the year 2000 goals, adopted at the 1990 World Summit for Children, can be readily assessed.

I believe these three chapters provide a good sense of where UNICEF has been, of its current priorities, and, to the extent possible, of where it is headed.

Ideas and knowledge have changed and expanded dramatically over the past 50 years. Accordingly, so has our ability to make children's lives better. The global community, almost unanimously, has committed itself to doing just that, as expressed in the words and ethos of the World Summit Declaration and the Convention on the Rights of the Child.

With renewed commitment, we shall work for the day when the Declaration and the Convention are transformed from articles of faith into expressions of reality for the lives and hopes of the world's children.

This is also my first *State of the World's Children* report as Executive Director, and I want to honour my remarkable predecessor, James P. Grant. With his indomitable and generous spirit, he moved us all towards a better world for children. I am sure the evidence of progress in many areas of children's lives would have pleased him, as would our pledge to promote the Anti-war Agenda set forth in this report.

Carol Bellamy
UNICEF Executive Director

The State of the World's Children 1996

I see the world gradually being turned into a wilderness, I hear the ever-approaching thunder, which will destroy us too, I can feel the suffering of millions, and yet, if I look up into the heavens, I think that it will all come right, that this cruelty, too, will end.

These are the words of a 15-year-old girl. They could have been written yesterday—by a child in Bosnia or Liberia, in Afghanistan or the Sudan. In fact, they were written more than 50 years ago in the Netherlands, by Anne Frank, who died shortly afterwards in a Nazi concentration camp.

In 1996, UNICEF marks its 50th anniversary. The organization was founded in 1946 in the aftermath of World War II, as the United Nations International Children's Emergency Fund. Times have changed—and they have not changed. In 1996, the world's children again face the carnage of war. Millions live with shattered innocence, daily terror and stifled hopes, which Anne Frank would recognize only too well.

This year, *The State of the World's Children* reflects the terrible symmetry of 1946 and today. Chapter I is a report on children in war—on their lives and on their deaths. Children thrown into mass graves. Children wandering without their parents or wasting away in refugee camps. Children brutalized into being killers themselves.

Chapter II of the report then takes a historical perspective. It looks at what has changed in the last 50 years. The thread of violence runs through this too, for communities and children suffering the silent emergencies of poverty and hunger. But there have also been enormous achievements.

Child mortality rates have fallen by about 50 per cent, and total annual child deaths have dropped dramatically from 25 million to 12.5 million.[1] Since 1980, basic immunization has saved the lives of about 20 million children.[2] As the second part of the report points out, there has also been major progress in the priority accorded to children. Officially at least, governments respect and value children as never before. The Convention on the Rights of the Child entered into force in 1990 and had been ratified by 179 countries as of the end of September 1995.

If children are loved and valued, why are they still being used as cannon-fodder? A weary response might lay the blame on innate human cruelty and duplicity. A cynic would also argue that incessant television coverage has done little more than stun our sensibilities, and that all conventions and declarations will inevitably crumple before the barrel of a gun.

UNICEF takes a different view. It believes that this gap between rhetoric and reality represents a historic challenge. In response to so much destruction and pain, there have also been unprecedented efforts at peacemaking and caring for the victims. The urgency now is to vastly enhance the means both to prevent future conflicts and to better support victims.

UNICEF argues that concern for children is one of those means. We believe that love and respect for children are key to humanitarian and political progress. Many of today's most intractable disputes, for all the ethnic or religious character they acquire, are at heart struggles for resources and for survival. Today's problems of poverty and violence will never subside unless we invest in the physical, mental and emotional development of the next generation.

Concern for children is also a way of addressing today's violence. Wars are not going to disappear overnight, but we can at least mitigate their effects and ensure that they do not target children and women. To that end, this report sets out UNICEF's Anti-war Agenda—a series of steps that we believe to be both realistic and effective and that would dramatically improve the well-being of children in situations of conflict. Vital measures here include removing child soldiers from the battlefields, and banning the manufacture of weapons such as anti-personnel land-mines that target civilians. Better information can also play a part: we can publicly recognize and systematically document genocide and instances of torture and rape to warn potential perpetrators that the world is watching—that there will be no impunity.

Beyond defending children, we should also use child protection as a means of opening up dialogue. The idea of children as 'zones of peace' has already proved its worth with temporary cease-fires to allow children in war zones to be vaccinated, or to allow food supplies to pass through enemy lines.

At the same time, we need to address rehabilitation. Many children have immediate needs for food or shelter. They also require psychosocial support—to help them recover from emotional wounds. Communities, too, require social rehabilitation. In many of today's chronic disputes violence does not cease, it merely subsides—sustained partly by the persistence of weapons and the pervasive military ethos. Avoiding future conflicts will require not just caring for the youngest victims of war, but also educating them for peace.

The Anti-war Agenda rests on the proposition that much of the tragedy befalling children is preventable. The evil deeds that this report documents are, after all, driven by human behaviour. Children are suffering as a direct and immediate consequence of the decisions of adults. If conflict seems, at times, to be inevitable, there is nothing inevitable about children bearing the brunt of its consequences. Brutality, violence, rape and torture—all would stop tomorrow if the will to stop them existed, or if the rest of us devised means to compel them to be stopped.

In so doing, the world would be living up to the fundamental purpose of the United Nations Charter: "...to save succeeding generations from the scourge of war."

Children in war

The establishment of the United Nations after World War II raised hopes of a new era of peace. This was over-optimistic. Between 1945 and 1992, there were 149 major wars, killing more than 23 million people. On an average yearly basis, the number of war deaths in this period was more than double the deaths in the 19th century, and seven times greater than in the 18th century.[3]

War and political upheaval have been tearing whole countries apart—from Bosnia and Herzegovina to Cambodia to Rwanda. And this vortex of violence is sucking in ever-larger numbers of children. Entire generations have grown up in the midst of brutal armed conflicts. At the end of 1995, conflicts have been running in Angola for over 30 years, in Afghanistan for 17 years, in Sri Lanka for 11 years and in Somalia for 7 years.

Children have, of course, always been caught up in warfare. They usually have little choice but to experience, at minimum, the same horrors as their parents—as casualties or even combatants. And children have always been particularly exposed. When food supplies have run short, it is children who have

been hardest hit, since their growing bodies need steady supplies of essential nutrients. When water supplies have been contaminated, it is children who have had the least resistance to the dangers of disease. And the trauma of exposure to violence and brutal death has emotionally affected generations of young people for the rest of their lives. Recent developments in warfare have significantly heightened the dangers for children. During the last decade, it is estimated (and these figures, while specific, are necessarily orders of magnitude) that child victims have included:

▶ *2 million killed;*

▶ *4-5 million disabled;*

▶ *12 million left homeless;*

▶ *more than 1 million orphaned or separated from their parents;*

▶ *some 10 million psychologically traumatized.*[4]

The increasing number of child victims is primarily explained by the higher proportion of civilian deaths in recent conflicts. In the wars of the 18th, 19th and early 20th centuries, only about half the victims were civilians.

In the later decades of this century the proportion of civilian victims has been rising steadily: in World War II it was two thirds, and by the end of the 1980s it was almost 90 per cent.[5]

This is partly a function of technology. Aerial bombardment

Entire generations have grown up in the midst of brutal armed conflicts. At the end of 1995, conflicts have been running in Angola for over 30 years, in Afghanistan for 17 years, in Sri Lanka for 11 years and in Somalia for 7 years.

Photo: One of the rights of children is to be protected from military conscription, but children have participated in a number of recent conflicts. Young soldiers from Myanmar drill.

Recently, in 25 countries, thousands of children under the age of 16 have fought in wars. In 1988 alone, they numbered as many as 200,000.

has extended the potential battle zone to entire national territories. World War II saw a massive increase in indiscriminate killings, with the bombings of Coventry and Dresden, for example, and the atomic bombs that were dropped on Hiroshima and Nagasaki. And this pattern was repeated in the Viet Nam war, which is estimated to have cost 2.5 million lives.

A further cause of the rising death toll for civilians is that most contemporary conflicts are not between States, but within them. Rather than being set-piece battles between contending armies, these are much more complex affairs—struggles between the military and civilians, or between contending groups of armed civilians. They are as likely to be fought in villages and suburban streets as anywhere else. In this case, the enemy camp is all around, and distinctions between combatant and non-combatant melt away in the suspicions and confusions of daily strife. In 1994, the UN Department of Humanitarian Affairs reported that 13 countries had ongoing "complex emergencies" of this type, and it classified over 20 million people as "vulnerable"; it also listed 16 other countries with potential emergencies.[6]

Families and children are not just getting caught in the crossfire, they are also likely to be specific targets. This is because many contemporary struggles are between different ethnic groups in the same country or in former States. When ethnic loyalties prevail, a perilous logic clicks in. The escalation from ethnic superiority to ethnic cleansing to genocide, as we have seen, can become an irresistible process. Killing adults is then not enough; future generations of the enemy—their children—must also be eliminated. As one political commentator expressed it in a 1994 radio broadcast before violence erupted in Rwanda,

"To kill the big rats, you have to kill the little rats."[7]

In these circumstances, classifying such processes as 'complex emergencies' is incomplete. To say they are complex is true enough, but this would cover most forms of human activity. It also obscures the fact that these are fundamentally political disputes. Even to say that they are 'emergencies' is optimistic, suggesting that they will soon be over. Rather, these are chronic forms of social conflict whose violent repercussions in the form of 'total war' could be felt for years or decades ahead.

Children as soldiers

Most child casualties are civilians. But one of the most deplorable developments in recent years has been the increasing use of young children as soldiers. In one sense, this is not really new. For centuries children have been involved in military campaigns—as child ratings on warships, or as drummer boys on the battlefields of Europe. Indeed the word 'infantry', for foot-soldiers, can also mean a group of young people. What is frightening nowadays is the escalation in the use of children as fighters. Recently, in 25 countries, thousands of children under the age of 16 have fought in wars.[8] In 1988 alone, they numbered as many as 200,000.

One reason for this is the proliferation of light weapons. In the past, children were not particularly effective as front-line fighters since most of the lethal hardware was too heavy and cumbersome for them to manipulate. A child might have been able to wield a sword or a machete but was no match for a similarly armed adult.

However, a child with an assault rifle, a Soviet-made AK-47 or an American M-16, is a fearsome match for anyone. These weapons

I dream of peace: The words of children in former Yugoslavia

UNICEF/C115-21

We are only twelve years old. We can't influence politics and the war, but we want to live! And we want to stop this madness. Like Anne Frank fifty years ago, we wait for peace. She didn't live to see it. Will we? —*Students from a fifth-grade class*

From the group, they chose the ones they were going to kill. They picked my uncle and a neighbour! Then they machine-gunned them to death. After that, the soldiers put the women in the front cars of the train and the men in the back. As the train started moving, they disconnected the back cars and took the men off to the camps. I saw it all!

Now I can't sleep. I try to forget, but it doesn't work. I have such difficulty feeling anything any more. —*Alik, 13*

A grenade had landed on our shelter. We had to climb over the dead bodies to get out. Meanwhile the snipers kept shooting at us.

My father was one of those wounded and was taken away to the hospital. We've not seen him since, but I hope that he is still alive, perhaps in one of the detention camps.

I try not to talk about these things, but I get so upset and keep having nightmares about what happened. —*Kazimir, 13*

I had a new tricycle, red and yellow and with a bell....Do you think they have destroyed my tricycle too? —*Nedim, 5*

I remember going to our apartment during an alert. When I entered the corridor, all the doors were closed. Slowly, I walked through the dark and opened the bedroom door. All at once, the sun shone brightly upon me. My sadness and fear completely vanished. But while I was enjoying it, I felt as if I had no right to such happiness. —*Ivan, 13*

So many people have been killed fighting for justice. But what justice? Do they know what they are fighting for, who they are fighting?

The weather is growing very cold now. No longer can you hear the singing of the birds, only the sound of the children crying for a lost mother or father, a brother or a sister.

We are children without a country and without hope. —*Dunja, 14*

No film can adequately depict the suffering, the fear and the terror that my people are experiencing. Sarajevo is awash in blood, and graves are appearing everywhere. I beg you in the name of the Bosnian children never to allow this to happen to you or to people anywhere else. —*Edina, 12*

Our teacher has told us about Anne Frank, and we have read her diary. After fifty years, history is repeating itself right here with this war, with the hate and the killing, and with having to hide to save your life.

"When I close my eyes, I dream of peace."

Aleksandar, 14, said this just after enduring a dressing change of the terrible burn wounds he suffered from a Molotov cocktail explosion. His words became the title of the book, *I dream of peace* (UNICEF/ HarperCollins, 1994), the thoughts and paintings of children recorded by UNICEF in the course of its programme to help children in former Yugoslavia deal with war-related psychological trauma.

Illustration: 'Wounded children in hospital', a drawing from I dream of peace, *by 14-year-old Suzana.*

A teenage soldier's story

UNICEF/95-0205/Pirozzi

Like many of his friends, Sergeant Lawrence Moore got ensnared in Liberia's civil war without stopping to think much about why. With children all over the country enlisting in militias, when he was 15 it just seemed the thing to do.

With the war over, Sgt. Moore, who gives his age as 20, entered Monrovia, the capital, for the first time. He rode in from the bush with his leader....

Strangely, though, for Sgt. Moore, like so many teenage fighters, their triumphal return to the capital has turned into a story of loss. Gone are the carefree years of adolescence. Gone, too, is the sense of purpose, even amid the horror, of the war-rior's life. But most of all, gone is any sense of hope about the future.

Unschooled and inarticulate, [the] young fighters rarely seem clear about why they joined the militia in the first place. One young fighter told of how [his militia] had killed his family... "But I joined them because they are the best."

Sgt. Moore, too, joined. "The first time I was sent to the front, I was so happy, because I found so many of my friends there...."

Like those earlier fighters, Sgt. Moore readily admits his impressionability. Wounded in the hand and foot in his very first combat, he told of how awed he had been to be taken to a field hospital for a week's treatment, a sign that for once he truly belonged to something....

Sgt. Moore, who was quickly sent back to the front, says, "We were losing a lot of men, but we killed a lot of them too, plenty. One night, one of my friends died right in front of me," he added. "I felt very bad, but I never stopped fighting. I said to myself, this is war."

As with so many other questions, when asked how many people he had personally killed, the young man with the gentle face said he didn't really know. "I killed so many on the battlefield, but never any civilians," he insisted. "When I killed my enemies, it felt good. But right now, I pray God to forgive me...."

Suddenly idle in Monrovia, with no clothes or money, another young fighter spoke with bitterness about how his leader's teenage son was already flying around town aboard a shiny motorcycle, while top officials already seemed locked in a best-dressed contest that mirrored their frenetic jockeying for power.

"When I think of the five years I spent in the bush, killing people and being shot at, I feel pretty stupid," the soldier said. "We were giving our lives for people who by tomorrow won't remember how they got where they are...."

That evening, the boy soldier, who was apparently being tailed by informers, was arrested. A payment secured his release and [a] reporter gave him some cash to flee the city. Asked what he would try to do, he answered with the only thing life so far has taught him. "My mother is in the United States," he said. "I will try to get to the United States and become a US marine." —by Howard W. French

---

Photo: A gun-carrying boy soldier is watched by other children in the Liberian town of Bong Mines.

are very simple to use. The AK-47 can be stripped and reassembled by a child of 10. The rifles have also become much cheaper and more widely available—having few moving parts they are extremely durable and have steadily accumulated in war zones.

Since their introduction in 1947, around 55 million AK-47s have been sold; in one African country, for example, they cost no more than US$6 each.[9] The M-16 is just as ubiquitous, and has been described by one military historian as the "transistor radio of modern warfare."[10]

Besides being able to use lethal weapons, children have other advantages as soldiers. They are easier to intimidate and they do as they are told. They are also less likely than adults to run away and they do not demand salaries.

In long-drawn-out conflicts children also become a valued resource. Many current disputes have lasted a generation or more—half of those under way in 1993 had been going on for more than a decade. Children who have grown up surrounded by violence see this as a permanent way of life. Alone, orphaned, frightened, bored and frustrated, they will often finally choose to fight. In the Philippines, which has suffered for decades from a war of insurgency, many children have become soldiers as soon as they enter their teens. When schools are closed and families fragmented, there are few influences that can compete with a warrior's life.[11]

Indeed, in these circumstances, a military unit can be something of a refuge—serving as a kind of surrogate family. In Uganda in 1986, the National Resistance Army had an estimated 3,000 children, many under 16, including 500 girls, most of whom had been orphaned and who looked on the Army as a replacement for their parents.[12]

At a more basic level, joining an army may also be the only way to survive. Many children joined armed groups in Cambodia in the 1980s as the best way to secure food and protection. Similarly, in Liberia in 1990, children as young as seven were seen in combat because, according to the Director of the Liberian Red Cross, "those with guns could survive." In Myanmar, parents volunteer their children for the rebel Karen army because the guerrillas provide clothes and two square meals a day; in 1990, an estimated 900 of the 5,000-strong Karen Army were under the age of 15.[13]

Finally, children may also have active reasons to want to fight. Like adults, they too may see themselves fighting for social justice—as was often the case in Central America or South Africa—or they may want to fight for their religious beliefs or cultural identity. In more personal terms, they may also be seeking revenge for the deaths of their parents, brothers or sisters.

Many children, therefore, want to become soldiers and offer themselves for service. Others are deliberately recruited. This was true in Liberia, where a quarter of the combatants in the various fighting factions were children—some 20,000 in all. Indeed, the National Patriotic Front of Liberia had its own 'small boys unit', ranging in age from 6 to 20 (Panel 2).

Armed groups will often aim their propaganda specifically at young people. In Sri Lanka, the Liberation Tigers of Tamil Eelam (LTTE) have been particularly active in the school system, indoctrinating children.

In these circumstances, children can be expected to join up. But even if they do not volunteer they may be recruited forcibly. Over the past decade, government forces in El Salvador, Ethiopia, Guatemala and

Children who have grown up surrounded by violence see this as a permanent way of life. Alone, orphaned, frightened, bored and frustrated, they will often finally choose to fight.

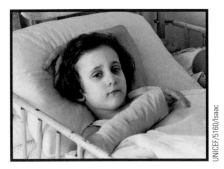

The fighting in Bosnia and Herzegovina has not spared the children. In Sarajevo, almost one child in four has been wounded.

Myanmar, among others, have all conscripted children. In the 1980s, the Ethiopian army would kidnap boys of 15 or younger from the villages and the poorest quarters of the cities, as well as from schools.[14] Opposition movements in many countries have also seized children—as in Angola, Mozambique, Sri Lanka and the Sudan.

The Renamo forces in Mozambique, in particular, systematically practised forced recruitment. Renamo had at least 10,000 boy soldiers, some as young as six years old. Similarly, in Angola, a 1995 survey found that 36 per cent of children had accompanied or supported soldiers, and 7 per cent of Angolan children had fired at somebody.[15]

Once recruited, children undergo varying degrees of indoctrination, often verging on the brutal. While in the early 1980s rebel groups in El Salvador offered primary school instruction, usually the training offered is less benevolent. Indigenous children in Peru, who have been forced to join guerrilla bands, have undergone long periods of forced political indoctrination. And others have suffered particularly brutal forms of induction. Some rebel groups in Cambodia and Mozambique turned children into fierce warriors by subjecting them to a brief period of terror and physical abuse—'socializing' them into violence. Much the same thing has been happening more recently in Sierra Leone, where in 1995 the Revolutionary United Front has been raiding villages to capture children into its ranks and force them to witness or take part in the torture and execution of their own relatives. Thus outlawed and brutalized, and often fed crack or other drugs, the children have been led to neighbouring villages to repeat the exercise.[16]

Children's actual duties in warfare cover the whole range of military activities. At relatively quiet times in camp this may be little more than cooking or carrying water. Being small and inconspicuous, children also have particular value as messengers or as spies. In Uganda in 1986, the National Resistance Army sent children into the capital to spot the government fortifications and when the shelling started, the children mingled with the fleeing crowds and threw handgrenades at trucks full of government soldiers.[17]

And while children might be thought to be the people deserving greatest protection, as soldiers they are often considered the most expendable. During the Iran-Iraq war, child soldiers, for example, were sent out ahead in waves over minefields.[18]

Torture and rape

Many children suffer appalling violence as soldiers, but even those who remain 'civilians' can be subjected to horrific experiences. Anything that can be done to adults, however monstrous, can also be visited on children. Children have been tortured as part of collective punishments for whole communities, or as a means of extracting information about peers or parents. They have also been tortured as a way of punishing their parents, or in some cases simply for entertainment. Once immersed in this savage environment, differences of age soon seem irrelevant.

This also means that children are as likely as adults to be captured and imprisoned. The treatment of child prisoners is a matter of increasing concern—particularly in Rwanda where, for the first time in history, children have been imprisoned and are facing trial for genocide.

In these violent circumstances,

women and girls in particular suffer the added trauma of sexual abuse and rape, which psychologists identify as the most intrusive of traumatic events. Without help, girls will carry the long-term effects of such abuse into their adult lives.

Sexual violence is particularly common in ethnic conflicts. In fighting in Bosnia and Herzegovina and Croatia, it has been deliberate policy to rape teenage girls and force them to bear 'the enemy's' child. A European Community fact-finding team estimated that more than 20,000 Muslim women have been raped in Bosnia since fighting broke out in April 1992.[19]

In Rwanda, rape has been systematically used as a weapon of ethnic cleansing to destroy community ties. In some raids, virtually every adolescent girl who survived an attack by the militia was subsequently raped. Many of those who became pregnant were then ostracized by their families and community; some abandoned their babies, others committed suicide. In the Renamo camps in Mozambique, young boys, who themselves had been traumatized by violence, frequently inflicted sexual violence on young girls—threatening to kill or starve them if they resisted.[20]

Even women and girls who are not physically forced to have sex may still be obliged to trade sexual favours for food, shelter or physical protection for themselves or their children.

The rise of sexually transmitted diseases, and particularly of HIV/AIDS, is therefore inevitable. One factor contributing to the high rate of AIDS in Uganda could be that some women had to trade sex for security during the country's civil war. As a result, the next generation is at an even greater disadvantage, as more children are born with AIDS or are orphaned.

Uprooted children

The waves of violence that have swept across the world in recent years have uprooted enormous numbers of people—at least half of whom are children. Some are classified as 'displaced', having fled their homes to move elsewhere within their own country; others are 'refugees' who have crossed borders into neighbouring countries. The total number of uprooted people is currently around 53 million—one out of every 115 people on earth has been forced into flight.[21] Since three quarters of refugees have fled from one developing country to another, this places an enormous strain on countries that already have problems caring for their own populations.

When forced into squalor and deprivation—the characteristic conditions of refugee camps—children are at particular risk. One of the most serious problems is malnutrition. In 1992, refugee populations in Somalia had mortality rates very much higher than during peace. There have been widespread outbreaks of micronutrient diseases such as scurvy, beri-beri and pellagra.[22] And in Angola, Liberia and the Sudan, the prevalence of wasting was more than 40 per cent. In the Goma refugee camp in eastern Zaire in 1994, a cholera epidemic killed 50,000 people in just one month.

Most refugee and displaced children travel with their families. But many lose their parents. 'Unaccompanied minors' typically account for up to 5 per cent of a refugee population, and often more—as children are lost, separated or orphaned in the panic of flight.[23] In Rwanda at the end of 1994, an estimated 114,000 children had been separated from their families.[24] In Angola, a 1995 UNICEF survey found that 20 per cent of children

Civil war in Rwanda separated some 114,000 children from their parents. Finding their families is a first priority for UNICEF.

In Somalia, during 1992, half or more of all the children under five on 1 January were dead by 31 December.

had been separated at some time from their parents and relatives.[25] Almost all separations are accidental, but some are deliberate. Haitians and Vietnamese, for example, have sometimes sent children ahead in boats in the hope that the whole family will find it easier to gain asylum.

One of the most disturbing cases of lost children has emerged in the civil war in southern Sudan. Apart from the main government and opposition groups, there are also various militias that spread terror by pillaging villages and killing or seizing their inhabitants. Fearing capture or death, at least 20,000 Sudanese young people, mostly boys between the ages of 7 and 17, have fled their homes. Thousands of girls have also been killed or abducted by the raiders, but few have run away from their villages since it is more difficult for girls to envisage life outside their families. These 'lost boys' of the Sudan have been trekking enormous distances over a vast unforgiving wilderness, seeking refuge from the fighting. Hungry, frightened and weakened by sleeplessness and disease, they have crossed from the Sudan into Ethiopia and back. Many have died on the journey; most survivors are now in camps in the parched northwestern plains of Kenya (Panel 3).[26]

Not all lost children will remain on their own for long. Many who have parted from their parents are subsequently taken in by members of their extended family or community. In Mozambique, a large number of the estimated 200,000 orphaned and unaccompanied children have been absorbed by extended families, or by members of former communities or ethnic groups.[27] Others are likely to end up in the cities. A 1991 study in Liberia found that over 90 per cent of those children surveyed who were living or working on the streets had been

there only since the war, and over half of them said they were there because they had been separated from their families.[28]

Famine and disease

Whether they are on their own or with their parents, most of the children who die in wartime have not been hit by bombs or bullets but have succumbed to starvation or sickness. In African wars, lack of food and medical services, combined with the stress of flight, have killed about 20 times more people than have armaments. One 1980 study in a war zone in Uganda attributed only 2 per cent of the deaths to violence—whereas 20 per cent were caused by disease and 78 per cent by hunger.[29] And when war is combined with drought, the death toll can be enormous: in Somalia, during 1992, half or more of all the children under five on 1 January were dead by 31 December—and around 90 per cent of these died from the interaction of malnutrition and disease.[30]

Most such deaths arise from disruption of the normal production and distribution of food. The manipulation of food supplies has always been a significant tactic of war but has been used particularly ruthlessly of late. For example, in the early 1980s, the Ethiopian Government used scorched-earth tactics to destroy hundreds of thousands of acres of food-producing land in Tigray.[31] And in Angola, the UNITA forces sowed large areas of land with anti-personnel mines to hamper food production in government-controlled areas, while mobilizing and relocating its own supporters to create food production bases. In many countries, grain stores have also been subject to attack by rebel and government forces.

War also hinders the distribution of food relief. Governments often

The lost boys of the Sudan

UNICEF/94-0858/Press

Since 1983, the Sudan People's Liberation Army (SPLA) and the Sudanese Government have been at war in southern Sudan. The conflict has already claimed more than 500,000 lives and displaced huge numbers of people. Among these were at least 20,000 children, mostly boys, between 7 and 17 years of age who were separated from their families. These 'lost boys' of the Sudan trekked enormous distances over a vast unforgiving wilderness, seeking refuge from the fighting. Hungry, frightened and weakened by sleeplessness and disease, they crossed from the Sudan into Ethiopia and back, with many dying along the way. The survivors are now in camps in Kenya, the Sudan and Uganda.

This extraordinary exodus has its origins in traditional forms of migration. After being initiated into manhood, young adolescent boys in southern Sudan have generally been quite mobile. Organized into small groups of their peers, they would leave home for a period to look after cattle. Or they might head for the towns or cities to go to school or to seek their fortune, before eventually returning home. In addition, at times of stress families all over Africa send their children elsewhere to find safety, food, work and schooling.

But during the war this process has escalated dramatically. Fearing they would be targeted as potential combatants, many boys left their villages and headed for cities such as Juba and Khartoum. Here they hoped to find work or schooling, though as these cities became saturated with migrants, the boys often had to resort to begging or petty crime.

Others set out for refugee camps in Ethiopia. Some travelled with friends or relatives, others slipped away on their own at night. Few had any idea of what lay ahead of them. They believed the trek would last only a few days and discovered that they faced a harrowing journey of 6 to 10 weeks. Continually under threat, they would flee for their lives, losing their way in the wilderness. Often they lost everything en route—blankets, sheets, shoes, clothes and pots—to soldiers, swindlers or bandits. Many fell victim to killer diseases. Others were so weakened by hunger and lack of sleep that they could go no further and sat down by the roadside—prey for lions and other animals.

The survivors who reached the camps in Ethiopia started to lead a relatively peaceful life. But it was not to last. Following the change of government in Ethiopia in May 1991 they had to flee again, back to camps in the Sudan. This time the journey was during heavy rains, and many perished crossing the swollen rivers or were hit by aerial bombardment. The luckier ones made it to a camp where they received help from the International Committee of the Red Cross.

This relative security was shattered again late in 1991 when fighting erupted around them, and they and children from other camps were on the move once more, eventually heading for Kenya.

Since 1992, UNICEF has managed to reunite nearly 1,200 boys with their families. But approximately 17,000 remain in camps in the region. The harsh memories remain as well. As 14-year-old Simon Majok puts it: "We were suffering because of war. Some have been killed. Some have died because of hunger and disease. We children of the Sudan, we were not lucky."

Photo: After years of separation, a Sudanese mother and son are finally reunited.

Sanctions: Children hard hit in Haiti

UNICEF/94-0780/Toutounji

To put pressure on violent or oppressive regimes the international community has increasingly resorted to economic sanctions. These may achieve long-term benefits, but they also cost lives—usually those of the poor and vulnerable.

Following the military coup in Haiti in September 1991, the United Nations imposed economic sanctions in an effort to restore democracy and human rights. Over the three years of sanctions, the rate of malnutrition for children under five increased from 27 per cent to over 50 per cent in many health institutions; thousands of children more may have died.

Before the overthrow of Haiti's first democratically elected government in 1991, the health of the nation's children was already among the most fragile in the western hemisphere, and most of the island's people, almost 7 million, lived in poverty. Sanctions caused employment and food production to plummet and also provoked inflation, which pushed up the cost of drugs and other essential items.

Primary school enrolment dropped almost 25 per cent, as parents could no longer afford to send their children to school. Many of the wealthy and powerful were sheltered by overseas bank accounts and could buy what they needed on the black market. The poor, however, had no cushion against additional hardship.

A six-member mission from the Harvard Center for Population and Development Studies went to Haiti in July 1993 and included a visit to Maissade in the Central Plateau. Save the Children had already reported from this rural area of 45,000 people that from 1991 to 1992, when sanctions were being enforced, child mortality increased by up to 64 per cent. They also reported that between 1990 and 1993 there had been a parallel increase in the proportions of children who were moderately and severely malnourished.

In addition to shortages of food, people also suffered from the deterioration in health services. Field interviews by the Harvard team revealed that shortages of drugs, supplies and electrical power had led to breakdowns in primary health care. Bottlenecks in public transportation also reduced access to health facilities. This led, among other things, to a decline in immunization coverage and a rise in deaths from measles and other infections. Between 1991 and 1992, the proportion of total deaths attributed to measles increased from 1 per cent to 14 per cent.

With the lifting of sanctions and the return of Haiti's President Jean-Bertrand Aristide in October 1994, a six-month-long measles eradication campaign, supported by UNICEF, immunized almost 3 million children between the ages of 9 months and 14 years, raising coverage to 95 per cent of children by August 1995. In comparison, only 20 per cent of children were covered in 1993. Many of those immunized also received vitamin A capsules and a dose of polio vaccine provided by Rotary International.

The Harvard team recommended that the international community sharpen its approach to sanctions. First, it should focus more precisely on the real targets: the military and their élite supporters—freezing overseas bank accounts, withdrawing commercial air traffic and denying visas. Second, it should take measures specifically to protect the poor. These would include guaranteeing free movement of life-saving supplies, especially of food and medicines; ensuring access to water, shelter and clothing for vulnerable groups, particularly for mothers and children; closely and impartially assessing and monitoring the welfare of innocent populations; and safeguarding aid from misuse and diversion.

Photo: Barefoot children run through water contaminated by garbage and sewage in a Port-au-Prince shanty town.

feed their armies first, distributing to the civilian populations only the food that remains. In Somalia in the 1980s, one estimate suggested that only 12 per cent of some food aid shipments reached the people for whom they were intended.[32]

Not only does war interrupt the distribution of food, but it also cuts supplies of water, with particular risks in cities. The long and devastating war in Lebanon had a very damaging effect on the quantity and quality of drinking water. One 1990 study found that 66 per cent of urban water sources were contaminated and that one third of urban communities were using cesspools for sewage disposal.[33] Water can also be a weapon of war. In Sarajevo, water systems have deliberately been destroyed to isolate and break down residential neighbourhoods; during the course of the war, 30 per cent of the pumping system and 60 per cent of the water mains' piping have been ruined.[34]

Communities at war also inevitably see attacks on their health infrastructure. In Mozambique, between 1982 and 1986, over 40 per cent of health centres were destroyed.[35] Health personnel are also often scattered, or may leave the country. In Uganda between 1972 and 1985, half the doctors and 80 per cent of the pharmacists abandoned the country in search of better opportunities elsewhere.

The lack of food, clean water and adequate health care in war zones exacts a terrible toll on children. For example, it is estimated that, in the period of conflict from 1980 to 1988, Angola lost 330,000 children and Mozambique 490,000 to warrelated causes.[36]

Sanctions

Many problems of nutrition and health can arise not just from military but also from economic war-fare—as the outside world tries to put pressure on errant regimes. While the United Nations finds itself caring for war-torn communities, the Security Council is imposing economic sanctions that create many of the same problems for the poor and vulnerable—leaving the real targets virtually untouched. The Secretary-General of the United Nations himself recognizes this dilemma. In June 1995, he described sanctions as a blunt instrument. "They raise the ethical question," he said, "of whether suffering inflicted on vulnerable groups in the target country is a legitimate means of exerting pressure on political leaders whose behaviour is unlikely to be affected by the plight of their subjects."[37]

The balance sheet of several years of sanctions against Iraq reveals a minimum of political dividends as against a high human price paid primarily by women and children. The food rationing system provides less than 60 per cent of the required daily calorie intake, the water and sanitation systems are in a state of collapse, and there is a critical shortage of life-saving drugs.[38] In Haiti, too, sanctions are thought to have cost the lives of thousands of children (Panel 4).

The trauma of war

Every conflict forces children to live through some terrible experiences. Indeed, millions of children have been present at events far beyond the worst nightmares of most adults. In Sarajevo, where almost one child in four has been wounded in the conflict, UNICEF conducted a survey of 1,505 children in the summer of 1993. It found that 97 per cent of the children had experienced shelling nearby, 29 per cent felt 'unbearable sorrow', and 20 per cent had terrifying dreams. Some 55 per cent had

It is estimated that, in the period of conflict from 1980 to 1988, Angola lost 330,000 children and Mozambique 490,000 to war-related causes.

Some 200 children 8 to 16 years of age, one third of whom were girls, were interviewed about their war experiences in a recent study carried out by the Christian Children's Fund. Two thirds of the children were natives of Huambo and Bie provinces; the rest were from eight other provinces. The interviews took place in schools, at camps for the displaced, on the streets and in orphanages. While the children selected were from a wide range of environments, they were not a representative sample. Nevertheless, the 200 interviews report traumatic experiences undoubtedly shared by many other Angolan children.

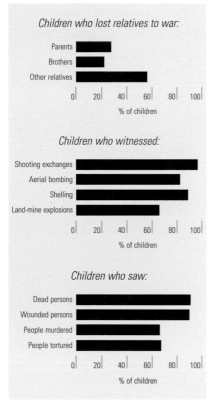

Children who lost relatives to war:

Children who witnessed:

Children who saw:

Source: Study by Christian Children's Fund, 1995.

been shot at by snipers, and 66 per cent had been in a situation where they thought they would die.[39]

Another survey in 1995 in Angola found that 66 per cent of children had seen people being murdered, 91 per cent had seen dead bodies, and 67 per cent had seen people being tortured, beaten or hurt. In all, more than two thirds of children had lived through events in which they had defied death.[40]

This type of experience can produce a range of symptoms. After the genocide in Rwanda in 1994, Dr. Albert Nambaje, clinical psychologist at the National Trauma Recovery Centre, reported: "Among the symptoms manifested by children are nightmares, difficulty in concentrating, depression and a sense of hopelessness about the future." The UN Commission on Human Rights' Special Rapporteur on former Yugoslavia similarly reports on interviews with children: "Memories of the event remain with them... causing extreme nightmares, daily intrusive flashbacks of the traumatic events, fear, insecurity and bitterness."[41]

It is universally true that horrific experiences are so deeply disturbing, so overwhelming, that a child will try to suppress bad memories rather than confront them. But many trauma researchers believe that it is the repression of memories and feelings that is at the heart of trauma suffering in both the short and long term.

Time does not heal trauma. A child must be helped to express suffering and to confront bad memories, with the support and guidance of an empathetic and informed adult. The very act of talking or writing about, or even acting out, traumatic events is a way for a child to begin healing and start on the road to recovery.

Every culture has its own way of dealing with traumatic experiences. In South-East Asia, studies of Cambodian, Lao and Vietnamese people show that each has very different conceptions of psychosocial distress. And much also depends on the family circumstances of the children, as well as on their age and the nature of their exposure to traumatic events.

In all cultures, one of the most important factors is the cohesion of the family and community, and the degree of nurture and support that children receive. Indeed, one of the most significant war traumas of all, particularly for younger children, is simply separation from parents—often more distressing than the war activities themselves.[42]

Adolescents also face particular problems. They are at a time of life when they are undergoing many physical and emotional changes. In some ways, they are even more vulnerable than younger children since they recognize better the significance of the events unfolding around them. Aid workers in Bosnia and Herzegovina have been encountering adolescents who have 'weeping crises', who attempt suicide, who are in a state of depression and who have increased levels of aggression and delinquency.[43]

Military expenditure— the opportunity cost

Even if they have never seen a gun, millions of children suffer from wars, as resources that could have been invested in development are diverted into armaments. Indeed, one of the most distressing realities of our time is that most wars have been fought in precisely those countries that could least afford them. In 1993, there were 42 countries with major conflicts and another 37 that were suffering from some kind of political violence. Of these 79 countries, 65 were in the developing world.[44] And military spending globally in 1993 was estimated to be US$790 billion, of which US$121 billion was spent in developing countries.

It seems clear that poverty and lack of development fuel hatred and escalate hostilities, and that improvements in such areas as nutrition, health, education, water, sanitation and family planning would go far to reduce the underlying causes of so many wars. The year 2000 goals for children, which call for an assault on poverty and underdevelopment through advancement in these areas, could be achieved for US$30 billion to US$40 billion a year more than is currently spent.

By any reasonable international perspective, this seems a relatively small sum of money. Consider the decline in military expenditures from 1987 to 1994: cumulative savings of nearly a trillion dollars.[45] This should have meant a transfer of sizeable sums of money to social, economic and environmental programmes. Instead, it appears that virtually all of these savings have gone to budget deficit reductions and non-development expenditures. This seems an extremely short-sighted policy.

At the same time, despite the overall global decline, large amounts of scarce resources continue to be devoted to armaments. Between 1960 and 1991, total annual military expenditures by developing countries rose from US$27 billion to US$121 billion.[46] Sadly enough, some of the steepest increases occurred in the poorest countries. Angola, Ethiopia, Mozambique, Myanmar, Somalia and Yemen have for many years spent more on their military than they have on their people's education and health. Money spent on arms could have been put to much better use. The United Nations Development Programme (UNDP) has estimated that

redirecting just one quarter of developing countries' military expenditure could have provided the additional resources to implement most of the year 2000 programme: primary health care for all, immunization of all children, elimination of severe malnutrition, provision of safe drinking water for all, universal primary education, reduction of illiteracy, and family planning.[47]

In recent years, however, there has been, as noted, some limited improvement in both developing and industrialized countries. As a result, a trend has emerged showing a global drop in military expenditures and an upturn in social spending (Figures 2, 3). Eritrea, Ethiopia, Mozambique, Uganda and Zimbabwe are examples of developing countries that have managed to reallocate their budgets.

Yet, distorted priorities remain and the industrialized countries must share responsibility since they are the dominant arms suppliers. The top five exporters to developing countries are the five permanent members of the United Nations Security Council. With the end of the cold war, the weapons industries in the rich countries are scrambling for new markets wherever they can find them—often with the enthusiastic support of their political leaders.

While arms sales have dropped significantly in the last few years, sales to developing countries in 1994 still amounted to US$25.4 billion, all of which is money lost to development efforts. The largest single supplier has normally been the US, though in 1994 France acquired that dubious distinction: its sales rose from US$3.8 billion in 1993 to US$11.4 billion in 1994.[48]

While these sales are largely of expensive hardware such as submarines or sophisticated fighter aircraft, much of the damage is now done by light weapons and smaller

Children are at particular risk from malnutrition because of war. A study in a war zone attributed only 2 per cent of deaths to violence; most are caused by the interaction of malnutrition and infection.

Fig. 2 Industrialized countries spending more on health and education, less on military

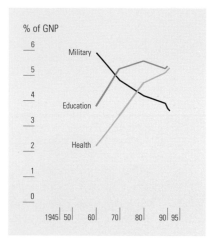

% of GNP

As a percentage of GNP, public spending on the military in industrialized countries has fallen by 40 per cent since 1960; health and education spending has been higher for at least 15 years.

Fig. 3 Public spending on military in developing countries outpaces health funding

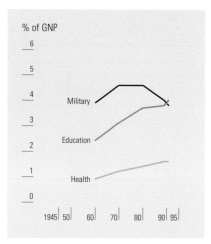

% of GNP

Military spending as a percentage of GNP has also declined in developing countries; expenditures on education almost equal those for the military. Health expenditures remain much lower.

Source for both figures: Sivard, R.L., *World military and social expenditures 1993*, Washington, D.C., 1993.

arms. Relatively little is known about the international trade in small arms, which often operates through the informal sector and powerful criminal networks. It is clear that in war zones weapons have been accumulating over decades. The arms on sale in the bazaars of Afghanistan, northern India and Pakistan, for example, are a legacy of the Soviet invasion of Afghanistan in 1979 and of the US pipeline of arms to the Afghan guerrilla groups. Similarly, the arms used in Somalia's civil war had been supplied to the previous regime by the US and the Soviet Union. And more recently, the arms used by the Government of Bosnia and Herzegovina include light weapons left over from the Lebanese civil war.[49]

It is therefore appropriate to repeat a tragically consistent theme in UNICEF reports on the state of the world's children: if even a fraction of the resources devoted to building military capacity could be diverted to achieving basic development goals, we would soon be living in a world with fewer social and environmental problems and far fewer and less destructive wars.

The legacy of land-mines

Of all the weapons that have accumulated over years of war, few are more persistent and more lethal to children than land-mines. Hundreds of thousands of children, herding animals, planting crops or just playing, have been killed or maimed by these deadly devices.

Since 1975, land-mines have exploded under more than 1 million people and are currently thought to be killing 800 people a month. There seems little prospect of any end to the carnage. In 64 countries around the world, there are an estimated 110 million land-mines still lodged in the ground—waiting.[50]

They remain active for decades. As one Khmer Rouge general put it, a land-mine is a perfect soldier: "Ever courageous, never sleeps, never misses."

There are basically two types of land-mines: anti-tank and anti-personnel. The most dangerous to children are the anti-personnel mines that explode even under the gentle pressure of a child's hand or foot. These come in a bewildering array of shapes and colours. Some look like stones, others like pineapples. But all can seem an interesting discovery for a curious child. One of the most infamous is the 'butterfly' mine, designed to float to the ground from helicopters without exploding, but with a shape and colour that also make it a deadly toy.

Virtually all combatants use land-mines. During the Persian Gulf war, the US and its allies laid about 1 million mines along the Iraq-Kuwait border and around the Iraqi city of Basra. And some 3 million have been laid in the continuing Balkan war. Some of the largest numbers lie in wait in Africa and Asia. The countries most devastated by land-mines are probably Afghanistan, Angola and Cambodia. Afghanistan has an estimated 10-15 million mines in place.[51] It is clear that many of these have been randomly scattered in inhabited areas precisely to cause civilian casualties and terrorize the population.[52]

Adults caught in the blast of an anti-personnel mine often survive with treatment, though they usually lose a limb. Children are less likely to survive because their bodies are so vulnerable. Those who do live will be seriously injured. A child may lose one or both legs or arms and sustain serious injuries to the genitals and abdomen. Shrapnel may also cause blindness and disfigurement. All of this happens in countries that have difficulty

Combating land-mines in El Salvador

¡ALTO!

UNICEF/93-1954/Robberts

In January 1992, peace accords between the Salvadorian Armed Forces and the Farabundo Martí National Liberation Front (FMLN) ended 12 years of bitter civil war. But while the guns had been silenced, the land-mines remained. Adults working in the fields and children picking up interesting-looking objects continued to become victims of war.

UNICEF brought the two parties together again a few months later to join forces against this continuing threat. One of the first priorities of this Mine Awareness and Accident Prevention Project was to try to locate the mines. Both sides provided maps, and within two months 425 minefields had been fenced off for public protection. Even so, the locations of many of the mines were unknown—the army had dropped some by air, and independent FMLN units had laid others but kept no records.

The second task was to warn the population. The army and the FMLN provided samples of their mines, and UNICEF produced thousands of posters that were dis-

tributed with illustrations of these devices and instructions on what people should do if they encountered a mine or any other unexploded device: "Don't touch. Mark the place. Turn around and leave the way you came. Tell the authorities."

The posters were reinforced by an education and public awareness campaign, through the press, television and radio. But each community also needed individual contact. A team of educators travelled around meeting teachers, health promoters and NGO staff. These volunteers were trained in mine awareness so they could serve as 'multipliers'—visiting rural communities, giving talks illustrated by flip charts and distributing leaflets to each family. Between October 1992 and December 1993, over 3,600 multipliers spoke to an estimated 300,000 people—representing 44 per cent of the population in high-risk areas.

These campaigns certainly brought the message home. One problem had been that farmers were removing the mine-warning signs because they desper-

ately needed the land to grow their crops. Others took the wooden stakes on which the signs were mounted to build furniture or use as firewood. After an intensive education campaign, all the stakes were replaced. The only casualties were the cattle that the farmers sent ahead to serve as mine detectors.

The other main component of the project was deactivating as many mines as possible. The Salvadorian Government hired a Belgian firm, which during 1993 and early 1994 deactivated a total of 9,511 mines. The company also trained 240 armed forces engineers and 240 FMLN members in mine detection.

As a result, the number of deaths attributed to land-mines and other explosives has fallen dramatically. In 1992, there were 579 victims; in 1993 this fell to 259, of which only one was attributable to a land-mine. Between January 1994 and May 1995, there was not a single reported accident involving a land-mine. There are, however, still risks from unexploded rockets, grenades, bombs and other devices. A second phase of the programme is now warning people of these dangers.

The mine clearance campaign has had strong local support. The Government has been committed to this programme and has borne the entire cost of mine clearance—more than US$4.8 million. The campaign has also benefited from a growing spirit of cooperation between two armies that were often deeply suspicious of each other. This successful programme, which combined mine clearance with mine awareness activities and education, will hopefully serve as a model for other countries afflicted by mines and living with this ever-present danger.

Photo: A young boy teaches younger friends how to avoid lethal land-mines.

offering the simplest medicines or pain-killers, let alone artificial limbs. In El Salvador, fewer than 20 per cent of child victims receive any kind of remedial therapy; the rest have had to fend for themselves as best they can—often begging or stealing to survive.

Land-mines cause enormous pain and suffering but they also bring lingering economic and social costs. In addition to the expense of medical treatment, and the cost to families of caring for injured relatives, they also hinder the flow of goods and people, and put huge areas of agricultural land out of production. In addition, the availability of land-mines contributes to the permanent 'militarization' of daily life. So common are they in Cambodia that they are now used for fishing, or as property security devices, or even to settle domestic disputes.

Land-mines can be cleared—but only laboriously and at enormous expense. Ironically, these weapons that can cost less than US$3 each to manufacture can cost up to US$1,000 each to clear. Trained workers have to crawl their way along, probing the soil ahead, inch by inch. One person can clear only 20 to 50 square metres per day.

The international community is slowly realizing the implications of a world studded with land-mines. Unfortunately, it has not been sufficiently shocked to take effective action. In 1993, it allocated only US$70 million for mine clearance in countries such as Afghanistan, Bosnia and Herzegovina, Cambodia, Croatia and Mozambique. In the same year, however, a further 2 million mines were laid—leaving a 'de-mining deficit' of 1.9 million mines, and adding some US$1.4 billion to the future cost of clearance.

Apart from the demand for mines from combatants, one of the major problems is that dozens of companies around the world, many of them household names, are still content to manufacture and sell these destructive devices. An increasing revulsion at this trade is encouraging a number of organizations to refuse to do business with companies involved in the sale or production of such weapons. Among United Nations organizations, UNICEF has joined the Office of the United Nations High Commissioner for Refugees (UNHCR) in supporting such a boycott.

At the time of the announcement of the boycott, Sadako Ogata, United Nations High Commissioner for Refugees, dealt with land-mines squarely: "For my part, I see little difference between those who use them and those who produce them....Whatever the present legality of manufacturing such weapons, the toll they take on innocent civilians amounts to a crime against humankind."[53]

A continuum of violence

It is shocking enough that children are blown up by mines, fighting on the front lines, or falling victim to famine or disease in refugee camps. But open warfare is only part of a much broader picture of violence against children.

Millions of other children struggle to survive in close-to-battlefield conditions on the streets of the world's cities—from Los Angeles to São Paulo to Manila. Guns and knives and fights are chilling parts of daily life. In the US, gang violence, often drug-related, is drawing in ever-younger children. In urban areas around the world, children spend their days begging or cleaning car windows—numbing their pain by inhaling chemical solvents or glue. And in some Latin American countries, businessmen have paid off-duty policemen, security guards, or professional killers to

Land-mines are catastrophic for children, whose small bodies are particularly vulnerable to the injuries they inflict. One of the most heavily mined countries in the world is Afghanistan.

UNICEF/5526/Isaac

eliminate street children they consider a nuisance.

Millions of other children suffer from the collapse of public services. The governments of many developing countries, in the face of deepening economic crises and under pressures of structural adjustment, have cut health and education services and reduced food subsidies. While there may be longer-term benefits to elements of adjustment, the costs to today's families and children have been immense.

This violent environment not only adds to human suffering, but also contains the seeds of future conflict. All of what are now seen as 'complex emergencies' have their roots deep in long-running social, political and economic crises. Even those disputes that appear most surprising have clear antecedents. The outbreaks of violence in Chiapas in Mexico in 1994 came as less of a surprise to those who lived there and knew of the sharp divide between the indigenous people of Chiapas and the rest of the country. Their state provides one fifth of the country's electricity and one third of its coffee, yet the Mayan population there lives close to destitution.[54]

Such pressures have built up over generations, but the world is clearly moving into a much more fluid era in which underlying tensions are erupting to the surface.

The collapse of communism, the end of the cold war and the extension of liberal democracy have all combined to create a much more volatile situation as people regroup in different political formations.

There is also greater economic uncertainty. The steady globalization of international finance and trade may be creating wealth for some, but for millions of others it is leading to conditions of marginalization and social disintegration. And industrialized countries have been increasingly reluctant to meet the financial shortfalls with aid. Development assistance actually fell in 1993 for the first time in several years. This is a particularly serious development for Africa, which finds it difficult to attract private funds.

Pointing out the chronic nature of many of these crises is not a counsel of despair. What it does, in fact, suggest is that unless these underlying issues are addressed, future generations of children will live in a constant state of war. The response has to take place at many levels simultaneously: legal, economic and political.

International protections

The world should, in theory, be in a stronger position to shield children since the principles of protection for children in wartime have been established in a number of international conventions.

A series of Geneva Conventions after World War I dealt with different aspects of the conduct of war by combatants. It was not until after the atrocities of World War II that the international community specifically addressed non-combatants and produced in 1949 another series of four Conventions, the last of which called for the protection of civilians in time of war (Fourth Geneva Convention, referred to below as 4GC). In 1977, this was supplemented by two Additional Protocols (referred to below as PI and PII) which provided children with special protection—dealing, for example, for the first time with their participation as soldiers. The issues covered by these treaties include:

▶ *General protection of civilians*—Civilians are entitled to general protection against the dangers from military operations. They shall not be the object of indiscriminate

In the destroyed Bosnian city of Mostar, a street sign alerting motorists to schoolchildren still stands, riddled with bullet holes.

UNICEF/94-0881/Lemoyne

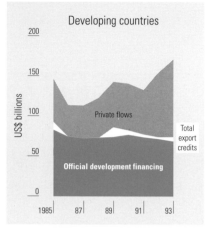

attack, acts or threats of violence (PI, article 51).

▶ *Supplies for children and mothers*—[Combatants should] allow the free passage of medical supplies, food and clothing for children, expectant mothers, maternity cases and nursing mothers (4GC, articles 23 and 55).

▶ *Starvation of civilians*—It is prohibited to attack, destroy, remove or render useless foodstuffs, crops, livestock, drinking water installations and supplies and irrigation works, etc. (PII, article 14).

▶ *Sexual exploitation*—Children shall be the object of special respect and shall be protected against any form of indecent assault (PI, article 77).

▶ *Unaccompanied children*—The parties to the conflict shall endeavour to ensure that children who have been separated from their families are not left to their own resources (4GC, article 24).

In 1989, a major new human rights instrument was introduced: the Convention on the Rights of the Child. This provides for much more complete protection of the child—defining standards of how children should and should not be treated. Indeed, the principles, the provisions and the procedures of the Convention are particularly relevant at time of war when all the rights of the child are at risk.

Articles of the Convention that are especially important in wartime include all those related to survival and to family support, as well as those concerned with education, health care and adequate nutrition. Other rights that are particularly at risk include rights to:

▶ *protection against exploitation and violence;*

▶ *protection against torture, or any other cruel, inhuman or degrading treatment or punishment;*

▶ *family reunification;*

▶ *a name and nationality.*

The Convention also makes specific mention of children in war. Article 38 calls on States Parties (i.e. governments) to apply the rules of international humanitarian law that are relevant to the child, and to take every feasible measure "to ensure protection and care of children who are affected by armed conflict."

Article 38 also urges governments to take all feasible measures to ensure that children under 15 have no direct part in the hostilities. Specifically with respect to child soldiers, it states:

States Parties shall refrain from recruiting any person who has not attained the age of fifteen years into their armed forces. In recruiting among those persons who have attained the age of fifteen years but who have not attained the age of eighteen years, States Parties shall endeavour to give priority to those who are oldest.

There was some controversy over this article in the drafting process. Many non-governmental organizations (NGOs), in particular, felt that the age limit was set too low. However, this debate has continued, and a United Nations working group has been established to draft an Optional Protocol to the Convention which would ban recruiting anyone below the age of 18.

Article 39 of the Convention also covers children in armed conflicts. It refers to the need for physical and psychological recovery and social reintegration of child victims.

Given the extent to which these principles have been flouted, it is easy to deride the existing body of international law. But these conventions are genuine landmarks. As late as World War II even the idea of extending any form of protection to enemy civilians was received with incomprehension. And the conventions do have some practical impact. While they may not prevent military abuses, they achieve some degree of restraint. Politicians who know that there are standards against which they can subsequently be judged are more likely to consider those standards in their calculations.

Clearly what is lacking, however, are the mechanisms and the will for enforcement. In some ways, enforcement has become more difficult in recent years. In the days when many conflicts were proxy wars, international agencies such as the International Committee of the Red Cross (ICRC) could make complaints not just to the combatants but also to Moscow or Washington. Now that these alignments have disappeared it is more difficult to apply external pressure. The issue is further complicated because the conventions apply to 'States Parties'. In today's armed conflicts, many of the offenders are not States at all but rather a loose collection of subnational groups, civilian and military, and in certain instances 'non-States Parties' have argued that they are not bound by the provisions of such conventions.

Nevertheless, many of the worst offenders are governments, and should be held to account. When politicians and military leaders know that retribution is not only possible but also likely, then the inhuman and impersonal decree of mass slaughter and genocide carries a much more personal dimension.

Encouraging compliance with international law requires first that any abuses are systematically monitored and that evidence is collected. It also requires a determination to prosecute offenders. Justice needs to be re-established if ordinary people are to have confidence in their reconstituted society. This is obviously difficult to do during the heat of conflict. And it is often even more difficult when the conflict is over and countries are desperate to

achieve national reconciliation. But granting immunity for war crimes comes dangerously close to condoning them. Along with war crimes there is also the issue of reparations for abuses suffered, for enforced prostitution of prisoners or for the physical damage suffered as a result of spraying chemicals such as Agent Orange.

The power of information

Today the world benefits from swifter and denser networks of communications—making it much more difficult to cover up abuses. At present there are some 145 commercial communications satellites carrying millions of conversations, data streams and news reports around the globe.[55] While in the Biafran war in 1967 it took two days for film about the war to travel from Africa to Western television screens, nowadays a reporter has to do little more than use a computer to send news and pictures back to base for instant onward transmission around the world.[56]

Yet the flow of information is far from perfect. The media are very selective about where they invest their time and money, and the cult of 'instantaneity' that technology encourages can flatten information into a homogenous stream of violent images and instant analysis. Nor is news reporting independent of the events under observation. Wars have always involved propaganda offensives alongside military ones. Much military strategy nowadays is directed towards capturing not just territory but headlines.

Aid agencies also get caught up in the media game. In Somalia, the first resort of most reporters unfamiliar with the events was to interview Western aid workers. Apart from often giving a one-sided picture, it raises the possibility that

Fig. 4 Net investments and assistance (continued)

Asia and Central and South America have benefited most from private flows. Sub-Saharan Africa, which does not attract much in private flows, has suffered a decline in overall terms.

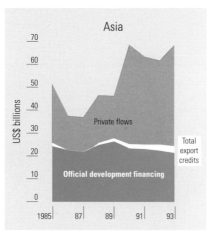

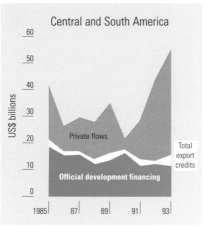

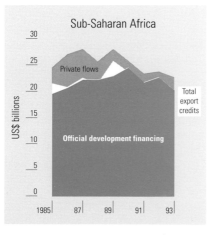

Source for four figures: OECD, *Development Co-operation—1994 report*, Paris, 1995.

How Sri Lanka educates children for peace

UNICEF/4822/Teixeira

Sri Lanka has suffered from a civil war for the past 11 years. This is a struggle that has permeated the life of the whole country, including the education system: most schools are now segregated along language lines, except for a few in urban areas.

To help children learn non-violent ways of resolving disputes, the Government, with UNICEF's help, launched a programme called 'Education for Conflict Resolution' (ECR). Initially, a core group of resource persons were trained at the National Institute of Education in some of the different forms of conflict resolution being used in other countries. They subsequently adapted these and developed their own methods appropriate to Sri Lanka—producing 10 different training manuals aimed at principals, teacher trainers, teachers and pupils.

Although some of the techniques were innovative, many of the ideas of conflict resolution struck familiar chords in Sri Lankan culture. For example, the methods of conflict resolution present aggression and passivity as two extremes and suggest that a better, middle, way is assertiveness. Buddhism, one of the major religions in Sri Lanka, is very much in sympathy with this: it, too, emphasizes the importance of taking the middle path. And Sri Lankan village life has traditionally operated on cooperative principles, so when the trainers suggest cooperative behaviour, it is more a question of helping people reinforce old skills, rather than teaching them new ones. The Buddhist and Hindu emphasis on harmony with the natural environment is also in tune with this approach.

Similarly, Hinduism and Buddhism make extensive use of meditation. ECR has incorporated meditation, though not for religious purposes; its aim, rather, is to calm and concentrate the mind to create a sense of inner peace. A typical lesson for primary schoolchildren, for example, would start with meditation, and then cover issues such as decision-making and conflict resolution. Role-playing is an important part of the approach, and children are encouraged to express emotions through stories, songs and poetry.

The focal point for training teachers in these principles is the Nilwala College of Education. Here, student teachers learn to integrate ideas and methods of conflict resolution into all subject areas. For example, a social studies lesson might focus on how different groups need to work together for a community to function. Within that lesson, students would be encouraged to act out a traditional story with a theme of peace and cooperation. In one such story, students pretend to be birds that have been captured by a boy with a net. When the boy goes home to find a sack in which to put the birds, they twitter with alarm at the prospect of being eaten and wonder what to do. Then one bird suggests that maybe they could fly away if they all worked together. The children then flap their arms like birds in flight and lift the net above their heads until everyone is free. Teachers learn to discuss the messages of stories with their students and help them to draw parallels between them and their own lives.

In 1992-1994, the ECR project trained 3,500 principals, 500 master teachers, 3,000 teachers and 7,500 student leaders, who in turn have reached approximately 420,000 of Sri Lanka's 4.5 million schoolchildren.

ECR is not limited to particular lessons on 'conflict resolution'; rather, it is integrated into the entire curriculum. Nor will ECR be confined to schools. In 1995, ECR began a media campaign to extend these ideas to parents and to the community as a whole.

Photo: Young Sri Lankans in school, where conflict resolution is part of the curriculum.

agencies may use publicity opportunities for fund-raising purposes.

Despite the reservations, modern media have certainly opened up channels that do allow both local people and international agencies the opportunity to get the information out and touch the world's conscience.

The possibilities for prevention

The underlying tensions that eventually erupt in violence are often easy enough to identify. As Peter Hansen, United Nations Under-Secretary-General for Humanitarian Affairs, recently noted, "Given our awareness of the circumstances and conditions which generate marginalization and vulnerability, exploit differences and exacerbate tensions, one need not be an Einstein to determine that tackling root causes is the only answer if we're serious about preventing conflict."[57]

An obvious way, then, to prevent conflict is to reduce tensions. It could be argued that the reason many countries have not fallen victim to widespread violence is precisely because they have pursued policies of more equitable development and effective social integration.

Malaysia, for example, is ethnically diverse. The majority are the indigenous Bumiputra population, but 30 per cent are Chinese and another 8 per cent Indian. Following race riots in 1969, the Government introduced clear policies to distribute the benefits of economic growth more equitably and thus reduce the potential for social tension.[58]

An effective way of reducing tension is to ensure equal opportunities for all children. Meeting their needs and investing in their healthy development is the foundation for more stable societies.

Children themselves of course have an important contribution to make—in trying to avoid the mistakes of their parents. Schools can foster these ideals through courses that allow children to explore ways of resolving disputes between individuals and communities that do not rely on violence. 'Education for peace' is often thought of as a form of reconciliation after war is over, but it also has potential for prevention (Panel 6).

Many parts of the world are already in an unstable situation where violence seems a likely outcome. In these circumstances, the international community needs effective early warning systems to permit speedy mediation. A number of international NGOs, notably the human rights organizations, perform a valuable service. However, receiving a warning and acting on it are two different matters.

As United Nations Secretary-General Boutros Boutros-Ghali has observed: "The whole idea of preventive diplomacy is something new and thus not readily accepted. It is like the introduction many years ago of insurance for your car. People were at first not ready to spend money on an accident that might never happen."[59]

After Rwanda, where serious observers still fear a renewed outbreak of genocidal strife, the contiguous country at high risk is Burundi, where the United Nations currently has people on the ground monitoring the situation. Thus far, the presence of the Secretary-General's Special Envoy and the deployment of human rights monitors, along with a mission from the Organization of African Unity, may have helped reduce the toll from ethnic fighting. Even in this case, however, the UN Centre for Human Rights has found it difficult to raise sufficient funds to pay for the monitors it needs.

Fig. 5 War and war-related deaths

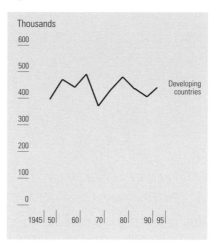

The number of deaths from wars and related causes has averaged around 400,000 per year for all developing countries, with little change between 1945 and 1992.

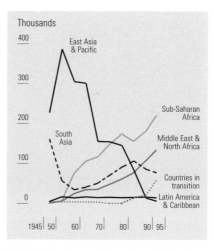

But the toll varies greatly by region, with deaths falling dramatically in East Asia and the Pacific from 1945 to 1992, but increasing in sub-Saharan Africa and the Middle East and North Africa during the same period.

Source: Sivard, R. L., *World military and social expenditures 1993,* Washington, D.C., 1993.

Note: Long-term trends in these charts were calculated using a moving average over several years.

33

Children as zones of peace

This report has focused on the increasingly damaging impact of warfare on children—on children as victims and combatants, on the ways in which international conventions have been flouted, and on the prospects for further deterioration as more and more States dissolve into sites of chronic violence. This is an area which will be further explored in the 'Study of the Impact of Armed Conflict on Children' by a high-level commission established by the UN General Assembly and chaired by Graça Machel, former First Lady of Mozambique (Panel 7).

The average viewer of the nightly news might not be too surprised at what is happening to children. War is seldom absent from our television screens. And the fact that all these things are being visited on children might be seen as yet another regrettable but inevitable aspect of humanity's capacity for violence.

But there is also a special reason for focusing on children. Most adults feel a particular shock and outrage when they see the bodies of children slain in battle or wasting away in refugee camps. They believe that children should somehow be above the political divide.

This concern is of more than sentimental value. It has frequently allowed relief to penetrate enemy lines to reach starving children beyond.

After World War I, Eglantyne Jebb, one of the founders of the British Save the Children Fund, who had organized food for needy children on both sides of the conflict, was charged in the United Kingdom with having given aid and succour to the enemy. "My Lord," she is said to have responded, "I have no enemies below the age of 11." She was acquitted.[60] Similarly during World War II, the establishment of what is now Oxfam was based on defiance of official opposition to aiding civilians in Belgium and Greece who were suffering from the Allied blockade.

UNICEF, too, as Chapter II of this report explains, has since 1946 frequently used its focus on children as a means of working on both sides in civil wars—as it did in the 1960s in Biafra, and later in the 1970s in what was then Kampuchea. However, it was not until the 1980s that the idea emerged of children as a 'conflict-free zone'—that children should be protected from harm and provided with the essential services to ensure their survival and well-being. That concept was first formulated in 1983 by Nils Thedin of Sweden in a proposal to UNICEF. If ever an idea seemed quixotic, this was it.

To expect the perpetrators of some of the most sadistic actions to stop and think about children initially made little sense. Until it was tried. Since Nils Thedin's proposal, a half-dozen corridors of peace, days of tranquillity, bubbles of peace—different names for the same phenomenon—have actually been negotiated in the midst of a number of bloody conflicts.

The first occasion was in El Salvador in 1985. After much negotiation with the Government and the rebels, there was finally agreement that the carnage should stop for three 'days of tranquillity'.

On three days in consecutive months, the Salvadorian conflict gave way to a campaign in which as many as 20,000 health workers immunized 250,000 small children against polio, measles, diphtheria, tetanus and whooping cough. This process was repeated every year until the end of the war six years later.

Similar principles have been

In the 1980s, the idea emerged of children as a 'conflict-free zone' — that children should be protected from harm and provided with the essential services to ensure their survival and well-being.

Impact of war on children: Study by high-level group

In late 1993, the United Nations Secretary-General, through a General Assembly resolution, launched a two-year study of the impact of war on children, to be headed by Graça Machel, former First Lady of Mozambique.

In an address to the UN in 1994, she promised that the study's report would be "uncompromising" in its candour. Speaking at a session of the Commission on Human Rights in Geneva, Ms. Machel said, "Violations of child rights and humanitarian law applicable to children are widespread and serious. Incidents of rape, torture, and the murder of child civilians mock the binding promises made by States in their adherence to the Convention on the Rights of the Child."

Ms. Machel is being supported by a group of eminent persons consisting of Hanan Ashrawi (Palestine), Belisario Betancourt (Colombia), Francis Deng (Sudan), Marian Wright Edelman (US), Devaki Jain (India), Rigoberta Menchu (Guatemala), Julius Nyerere (Tanzania), Lisbet Palme (Sweden), Wole Soyinka

(Nigeria) and Archbishop Desmond Tutu (South Africa). Support for the study is coming from all parts of the UN system, with UNICEF and the Geneva-based Centre for Human Rights playing lead roles. There is also a worldwide network of participating NGOs.

The group is undertaking a series of regional consultations in Africa, Asia, Europe, Latin America and the Caribbean and the Middle East, making field visits to several affected countries and commissioning a significant number of research papers.

The first of two African consultations took place in Addis Ababa in April 1995. Participants noted the "totality" of today's wars, in which political leaders manipulate accidental distinctions of race, class or ethnicity—forcing the participation of every man, woman and child. Some were concerned about confusion regarding the UN mandate to intervene when governments are unwilling or unable to protect the rights of their people. The meeting agreed that all warring parties must stop

recruiting or otherwise using children to achieve military objectives; demobilize child soldiers and integrate them into civilian life; protect non-combatants in areas of conflict, especially children and women; protect traditional sanctuaries, such as schools, hospitals and churches, and stop their selection as military targets.

The group will present its findings and a series of recommendations to the United Nations General Assembly in 1996.

"All of us," says Ms. Machel, "find it hard to believe that at the end of the 20th century, children are targets, children are expendable, children are victims, children are refugees, and even perpetrators—in one conflict after another, on virtually every continent."

She also believes, however, that there is a way out of the crisis. "I am under no illusions about the size of the task. But with the necessary political will, substantial progress can be made towards our common goal of making the rights of children in situations of armed conflict the rule rather than the exception...the task that we face is indeed a challenging one. But the cost of failure—for this generation's children and the next—is simply too high to bear."

Photo: A mother and her 10-year-old amputee son in Mostar are victims of modern warfare.

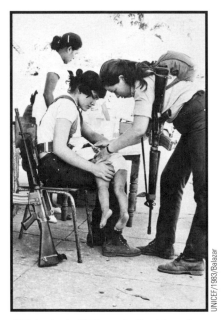

El Salvador in 1985 saw the first 'days of tranquillity', when the fighting stopped for three days to allow 250,000 small children to be vaccinated.

UNICEF/1983/Balazar

applied in other disputes. In 1986, in the war between the Ugandan Government and the National Resistance Army, the warring parties agreed to allow vaccines, personnel and equipment to travel along a corridor of peace. A few months later in Lebanon, in March 1987, hostilities were suspended for three days to permit all young children to be vaccinated. Two years later in Afghanistan, in 1988-1989, vaccination teams operated in both government- and mujahidin-controlled territories and in some areas raised vaccination levels above 80 per cent.

Probably the most sustained example of humanitarian aid working on both sides of a conflict has been in the Sudan. The Sudan for years had been racked by civil war, but during 1988 this had been compounded by a disastrous drought causing the loss of 250,000 lives and displacing nearly 3 million people. By January 1989, it was clear that a similar tragedy lay in store for the following year. The Secretary-General asked UNICEF Executive Director James P. Grant to meet with the warring parties—and Operation Lifeline Sudan (OLS) was the result. Through OLS the relief agencies negotiated both with the Government and the rebel Sudan People's Liberation Army (SPLA), which agreed to allow eight 'corridors' of relief to be created.

In the face of enormous odds, OLS achieved significant results. By the end of September that year, it had delivered over 100,000 metric tons of food and 4,000 tons of medical supplies.[61] At the same time, vaccination clinics became operational in all the garrison towns and reached 90,000 children in SPLA areas.

OLS also brought about a reduction in the fighting—at least along the corridors of tranquillity. It allowed people to move about the

countryside, and above all it gave people hope. Even after hostilities were resumed, civilian despair was never again to be so widespread or intense. A second phase was negotiated in March 1990 and, within the limits imposed by the fighting, has been running ever since. In 1995, the SPLA became the first combatant group in dispute with a recognized government to commit itself to abide by the provisions of the Convention on the Rights of the Child.

A new age of development uncertainty

The experience in the Sudan illustrates a pattern that is currently being replicated in many countries in Africa, the Middle East, the Balkans and Central Asia. In the past, civil wars usually ended with outright victory by one side. Nowadays, however, the conclusion is less clear cut. War and peace have an uneasy coexistence: fighting may stop in one place but linger sporadically elsewhere. And even after peace is declared, fighting may flare up again at any time.

This blurring of the distinction between war and peace is matched by a corresponding ambiguity in the programmes of aid agencies—uncertain about whether they should be aiming for short-term relief or long-term development. Most agencies have long agonized about seeing their long-term objectives interrupted by demands that they respond immediately to emergencies. These chronic conflicts are adding new dimensions to this conundrum.

At first glance, it does look as though the answer has simply been to increase relief. At the global level, the proportion of official development assistance devoted to emergencies has certainly been rising. And while in the early

1970s, much of this assistance was on a government-to-government basis, an increasing proportion of emergency aid in recent years has been passing through NGOs and the United Nations agencies. UNICEF's expenditure on emergencies between 1987 and 1993 rose from 7 per cent to 28 per cent, before declining slightly in 1994.[62]

These statistics are based on a supposedly clear distinction between emergency relief and development aid. However, these categories are often blurred. It is not clear that immunizing a child in a refugee camp counts as relief rather than development. And a borehole sunk near a refugee camp could later be used by the local community—and thus be seen as investment in rural water supplies.

In the case of chronic conflicts there is a further reason to set such categories aside—and reject the notion of relief first, development later. When the emergency is a climatic disaster, relief agencies work on the assumption that normal government services will later be resumed. In long-standing, conflict-related emergencies this assumption breaks down because a central element of the crisis is that many forms of governance have totally collapsed. In developing countries where the State is already weak, endless years of strife have only served to further undermine already frail public services.

In these circumstances, it is vital that relief does not inhibit recovery. Massive flows of emergency aid controlled by outside agencies may be the only way of feeding people in time. This form of assistance could displace already weakened government services and further compound the crisis. Relief and development activities ideally should be pursued simultaneously—and both should be seen as opportunities to build long-term capacity.

In politically complex and ambiguous circumstances, this is difficult to achieve but by no means impossible. It does, however, mean carefully assessing the strengths and weaknesses of existing institutions and making the best use of them. In Haiti, UN agencies and NGOs were able to make some contribution to development, but not in any way that would strengthen the illegal regime. Obliged to bypass the Government, they were nevertheless able to arrange for considerable amounts of food, fuel, water and medical supplies to be directly managed and controlled by communities and churches. This sustained capacity at the community level helped pull Haiti through its initial period after the restoration of democracy.

War relief for children

Healing the wounds of war-torn societies is a long and difficult undertaking. The immediate demand is to ensure that people, and especially children, are adequately fed, have access to safe water and are protected against disease. But recent experience has underlined the importance of five other tasks: caring for unaccompanied children; demobilizing child soldiers; healing the mental wounds of war; restarting schools; and embarking on education for peace.

▶ *Unaccompanied children*—One of the most urgent tasks is attending to the needs of unaccompanied children. In 1994, an estimated 114,000 Rwandese children were lost, abandoned, orphaned or otherwise separated from their parents. Some 70,000 were displaced within Rwanda, while most of the remainder crossed the border into Tanzania or Zaire. Many of these children were taken in by other families— some families took up to 9 or 10 children. Some children ended up in

Relief and development activities ideally should be pursued simultaneously— and both should be seen as opportunities to build long-term capacity.

One of the most significant war traumas for children is separation from parents, and the primary concern must be to reunite children and families. After six months' separation, two children in Rwanda embrace their mother, who cries as she holds them.

makeshift centres or former orphanages. Others ended up in special centres set aside for unaccompanied children in refugee camps. One of the risks of offering specific facilities for such children, however, is that their parents may be tempted to deliberately abandon their children in the hope that they will be better cared for by others.

The ultimate aim, of course, should be to reunite children with their families. In Rwanda, Save the Children, UNICEF, UNHCR and other partners have arranged with ICRC to standardize the process of data collection and tracing. This has included working with the Kodak company to enter photos of the children along with their details into computers and distributing printouts throughout the refugee camps. This kind of activity can be supplemented with information broadcast by radio. ICRC and the British Broadcasting Corporation have launched this type of tracing programme in Uganda. And the organization Doctors Without Borders has a similar programme with Radio Agatachya in Zaire. If the parents cannot be found, then members of the extended family are sought. Failing this, attempts are made to arrange for fostering or adoption by families from the same cultural group. Placing a child in an orphanage should only be a last resort.

▶ *Demobilizing child soldiers*— Child soldiers may find it particularly hard to emerge from war and build a new life. Many will have lost their families or have been forced to terrorize their own communities, making it impossible to return home. They may also find it difficult to live without the power that wielding a gun can bring, and will be tempted to drift into violence and crime. However, efforts are being made to demobilize child soldiers in a number of countries, including Liberia, Mozambique and

Rwanda. Some children are held first in transit camps to help them adjust to peace before returning to their communities and perhaps to school. Others are being offered training so they will have a more realistic chance of employment.

▶ *Healing the mental wounds*— Many child soldiers will have undergone horrific experiences that will live with them for the rest of their lives. For these, and many other children, one of the most important aspects of postwar development is psychological rebuilding.

Given the numbers of people affected, this task may seem daunting. But in recent years, much more has been learned about what can be achieved even with limited resources. In the past, treatment has concentrated on Western models using large numbers of highly paid staff to counsel individual children. While this may have helped a few children, it has proved far too slow and expensive a process to deal with the scale of the problem. It also has the drawback that Western advisers may know little about the local culture.

A better alternative is to train local people who can develop community-based approaches. Thus in Rwanda in 1994-1995, more than 2,000 Rwandese were trained as counsellors and caregivers. As a result of this work, around 70,000 people have participated so far in 'expression activities', such as singing, dancing, drama, drawing and writing, to ease the pain of their memories. Similarly in Bosnia and Herzegovina and Croatia, local professionals have been trained to screen children and identify symptoms of post-traumatic stress.

The long-drawn-out insurgency war in the Philippines has also been a traumatic experience for many children. There, it has been found that adults often avoid talking about violent incidents with their children because they find it too painful. They also tend to underestimate the damage done to children. In this case, too, it has been found that children have to be encouraged to express their pain in the ways with which they are most comfortable—through art or drama or gentle conversation.[63]

▶ *Restarting schools*—Another loss for children during wartime is the collapse of the education system. In Mozambique, damage to the education infrastructure left two thirds of the 2 million primary school age children without access to education.

A good way of returning children's lives to some semblance of structure and routine is to restart education as soon as possible. This does not require formal buildings or courses; education can be restarted even in refugee camps. In Rwanda, tens of thousands of children were able to start primary classes within two months of the end of hostilities through 'school in a box', a collection of basic supplies and materials for learning.

In Bosnia and Herzegovina and Croatia, international agencies have made great efforts to help local authorities reopen schools, even in the worst situations. In Sarajevo during the siege, individual dedicated teachers continued classes in their homes, in basements, or in other safe places, until schools were officially restarted in March 1993. In east Mostar, where there has been no electricity, children have been studying by candlelight with only the most basic materials.[64]

Attending classes, in whatever surroundings, can help children start the process of recovery, healing and reconciliation. In addition to conventional school lessons, they can be taught simple survival techniques, the dangers of minefields, and conflict resolution.

In Liberia, readmission to local schools lies at the hub of a demobilization programme for child soldiers, which draws on community-based rehabilitation initiatives, vocational training centres, drop-in centres and halfway houses.

▶ *Education for peace*—When schools are functioning there is also the opportunity to make a longer-term contribution through 'education for peace'—allowing children to develop mutual understanding, to resolve differences without recourse to violence and to show how human diversity can be embraced rather than become the basis for barbaric behaviour.

In Lebanon in 1989, UNICEF negotiated with a number of armed factions to transport children from different religious and cultural backgrounds to a two-week summer camp. Through sports, creative workshops and other activities, the children were invited to question their values, beliefs and biases while learning conflict resolution skills. Since then, more than 240 NGOs have undertaken education for peace activities, and the Lebanese Government has included peace education in the national curriculum.

Education for peace has also been taken up in other countries. In Liberia, a Children's Peace Theatre has been touring since 1992, promoting unity and reconciliation. In Mozambique, a Peace Circus uses art, dance and theatre to demonstrate that differences do not have to be settled at the point of a gun.

Though the underlying purpose of all of these programmes is the same, they have to be developed by people in affected communities to match particular cultural needs and circumstances. Many of the same principles are also being applied in schools in a number of other countries to counter racism and animosity towards immigrants and to foster the value of tolerance.

UNICEF and NGOs work together to help child refugees—starting with vaccinations and checking children's weight-for-age. Growth monitoring is vital for detecting malnutrition, which, even when mild, threatens children's lives.

Anti-war Agenda

The plight of children in war-time contradicts not just every normal human concern for their welfare but also the professed beliefs and legal obligations of those responsible. It might be easy to dismiss this contradiction as callous hypocrisy. UNICEF sees it rather as a challenge. We believe that insisting on the rights of children is one of the best ways of reasserting core humanitarian values. In the words of Graça Machel, "Despite the inherent brutality of conflict, no one can possibly believe it is ever permissible to murder, rape, torture or enslave children." Nor is it permissible to stand by and allow it to happen.

We do not argue that our Anti-war Agenda is some grandiose initiative to bring peace in our time. We do argue, however, that it is a vital beginning. And what gives it particular legitimacy is the existence of the Convention on the Rights of the Child.

The Convention is the guiding force of the Anti-war Agenda and we are determined that warring parties in any conflict be aware of, and be obliged to apply, the protections for children that the Convention provides. We will strive to ensure that the principles of international human rights law are observed to the full when the lives of children are at stake—whatever is needed, be it training of the military in various countries, training for UN peace-keepers or training for international NGOs.

UNICEF believes—along with many colleagues from governments, humanitarian agencies and NGOs—that the following agenda is vital:

Prevention

The world must no longer wait for the outbreak of hostilities before it pays heed. Much more deliberate effort should be made to address the underlying causes of violence and to invest more resources in mediation and conflict resolution.

Girls and women

In the midst of conflict, specific community-based measures are necessary to monitor the situation and needs of girls and women and especially to ensure their security because of the terrible threat they face of sexual violence and rape. Traumatized girls and women urgently need education and counselling. Because in times of conflict women's economic burdens are greater, access to skills training, credit and other resources must be secured. Education, women's rights legislation and actions to strengthen women's decision-making roles in their families and communities are all needed, both before and after conflicts.

Child soldiers

UNICEF believes that the minimum age of recruitment into the military should be 18 years. At present, under the Convention on the Rights of the Child, it is 15 years. The change could be achieved through the adoption of an Optional Protocol to the Convention. Beyond that, there is a great need to concentrate on rehabilitating child soldiers to prevent them from drifting into a life of further violence, crime and hopelessness.

Land-mines

No international law specifically bans the production, use, stockpiling, sale and export of anti-personnel mines. It is now time for such a law. UNICEF joins many other organizations in concluding that this is the only way to stop the endless suffering of children and other civilians. UNICEF will not deal with companies manufacturing or selling land-mines.

War crimes

Recent years have seen the most barbaric acts of violence against children and other civilians. These must be denounced as they are revealed. International war crimes tribunals must have both the support and the resources to bring perpetrators to justice.

Children as zones of peace

This idea should be pursued more vigorously. The gains from establishing such zones may be fragile and temporary. Nevertheless, zones of peace have become an important part of international diplomacy—capable of prising open vital areas of humanitarian space in even the darkest conflicts. As such, UNICEF intends to pursue the possibility that zones of peace be raised to a tenet of international humanitarian law.

Sanctions

Economic sanctions are imposed on the assumption that the long-term benefits of pressure on errant regimes outweigh the immediate cost to children. This may not be the case. There should be a 'child impact assessment' at the point at which any set of sanctions is applied, and constant monitoring thereafter to gauge impact.

Emergency relief

In situations of long-term conflict, aid should be seen as part of a process to help rebuild a society's capacity and promote development.

Rehabilitation

A much more deliberate effort needs to be made to demobilize both adult and child soldiers and rebuild communities so as to offer not just respite but also reconciliation. An important part of rehabilitation must be to address the psychosocial damage that children suffer.

Education for peace

Disputes may be inevitable, but violence is not. To prevent continued cycles of conflict, education must seek to promote peace and tolerance, not fuel hatred and suspicion.

UNICEF is committed to mobilizing whatever resources are necessary in pursuit of these goals wherever conflicts break out. It is the singular characteristic of warfare in our time that children suffer most. But that only makes the task more urgent. Without minimizing the difficulty, we are confident that children's needs can be met even in the midst of the inferno of war. However dreadful the armed conflict, the death and suffering of children cannot be tolerated.

Children need be the victims of war only if there is no will to prevent it. Experiences in dozens of conflicts confirm that extraordinary actions have been taken and can be taken to protect and provide for children. Our Anti-war Agenda is intended to expand the scale and scope of those efforts, and we will direct much of UNICEF's future activities to this all-important end.

Fifty years for children

The creation of the United Nations in 1945 represented the coming of age of an ideal of international cooperation. Its immediate spur was the destruction caused by World War II, but behind this lay a longer-term desire to promote world peace. There was, however, no idea of setting up within the constellation of new institutions a special organization for children. The creation in 1946 of the United Nations International Children's Emergency Fund was an accident of early cold war politics.

The prospects in Europe were grim. The winter of 1946-1947 was particularly bitter. Millions of people were still without proper shelter, fuel, clothing or food. Children especially were suffering: in some affected areas, half of all babies were dying before their first birthday. The Allies, anticipating widespread devastation at the end of the war, had established the United Nations Relief and Rehabilitation Administration (UNRRA) in 1943 to provide general assistance. But the Iron Curtain descended, and the United States Government refused to go on using UNRRA as a relief channel because it was aiding countries in both Western and Eastern Europe.

Photo: Children of Greece. UNICEF was set up to meet the emergency needs of children when famine threatened parts of Europe in the aftermath of World War II.

Just as UNRRA was about to be wound up, however, voices were raised at its final meeting in Geneva to protest the fate of Europe's children. The delegate from Poland, Ludwik Rajchman, was particularly vocal, and the meeting accepted the proposal that UNRRA's residual resources should be put to work for children through a UN International Children's Emergency Fund—an 'ICEF'. Rajchman was regarded, therefore, as the founder of UNICEF. The Executive Director designate, Maurice Pate, made it a condition of his service that there were no caveats about where the aid (mostly dried milk) might go, insisting that UNICEF support equally children in vanquished as well as victorious countries. Subsequently, on 11 December 1946, a resolution of the UN General Assembly—number 57(I)—brought UNICEF into being. Fortuitously, therefore, the Children's Fund became part of that continuing experiment in international cooperation that has since constituted the United Nations system.

Coincidentally and almost unnoticed, the international community had also embraced the new central principle: that children were above the political divide.

This was quickly put to the test. Some of the most important early programmes supported by UNICEF were established in East European

The winter of 1946-1947 was particularly bitter. Millions of people were still without proper shelter, fuel, clothing or food. Children especially were suffering: in some areas, half of all babies were dying before their first birthday.

From the beginning, UNICEF has helped feed hungry children wherever they are, supporting all children equally.

ICEF-0244

countries—Poland, Romania and Yugoslavia—as well as Germany. And in the late 1940s, UNICEF provided relief assistance on both sides of the civil wars in China and Greece. It also sent aid to children in the Middle East uprooted by the creation of Israel.

UNICEF was established to help children damaged by war. But it stayed in existence to take on a much broader role. While UN Member States had not intended to prolong UNICEF's life beyond the postwar emergency, they did include in its founding resolution the phrase "for child health purposes generally," and this was to offer the Children's Fund a permanent niche in the large-scale control and prevention of diseases affecting children.

When the time came in 1950 for the UN to close down its 'ICEF', a successful lobby was mounted to save it. This time, it was the new nations of the 'developing' world that spoke up. How, asked the delegate from Pakistan, could the task of international action for children be regarded as complete when so many millions of children in Africa, Asia and Latin America languished in sickness and hunger, not because of war, but because of the age-old problem of poverty? Again, the plea did not go unheard. This was the first turning-point in UNICEF's history. In 1953, the General Assembly confirmed the children's organization as a fixture in the UN system.

UNICEF at this time dropped 'International' and 'Emergency' from its title—becoming simply the United Nations Children's Fund (although retaining its acronym). But it never abandoned the children of crisis—those affected by war, conflict, drought, famine or any other emergency. However, its mission expanded as the post-colonial era presented it with a new challenge.

In the late 1950s and early 1960s, the winds of change were to blow away most of the remaining colonial order in Africa and the Caribbean. And at the United Nations, US President John F. Kennedy urged an end to the poverty in the newly independent countries of the developing world. UNICEF took up that challenge on behalf of children. This was the second major turning-point in UNICEF's history.

The 'development' era redefined the children's cause. Children previously had been seen as objects of purely humanitarian and welfarist concern—as 'children in distress' or as 'children in poverty'—to be taken into care or given supplementary support. Like refugees, the elderly or the disabled, children were regarded as a special group. But according to the new development perspective, children were not another cause. They were part of every cause. Among the hungry, the sick, the ill-fed, the poorly clothed, the homeless, the jobless, the illiterate and the destitute, there were always children. And unless they were orphaned or abandoned, children could never be treated in isolation from their parents and families, and especially not from their mothers.

From this perspective, a mission on behalf of children was no longer neat and self-contained. Helping nations to help their children demanded engagement in many areas of human activity. It certainly involved creating services to help children directly, such as maternal and child health, early childhood care and primary education. But it also demanded others that were not specific to children, such as water supplies and sanitation, slum and shanty town renewal, and credit facilities for women entrepreneurs.

The same breadth of concern also extended to policy. Any issue that affected whole communities also affected their children—agriculture, industrialization, population growth, women's rights, environmental depletion and urbanization. The list grew steadily—later including debt, structural adjustment and the post-cold war transition. And always present or waiting in the wings were the multiple predicaments of disaster and conflict.

The response to the problems of children thus evolved into a subset of the growing post-colonial 'science' of development, and the quest to eradicate poverty. Within this broader pursuit, however, UNICEF argued that children had to be singled out because they suffered the most acutely from poverty. As a result, they were also poverty's most sensitive barometer.

Down the years, the UNICEF response to children's needs underwent many changes. In the 1950s, it involved mass campaigns against the menace of epidemic disease: tuberculosis, yaws, trachoma, leprosy and malaria. In the 1960s, the development movement emphasized the miracles to be wrought by transferring capital and technology from rich countries to poor and by investing in human capital, including children—'our most precious resource'. In the 1970s, doubts about development experience grew more prominent, and disillusionment with the pursuit of economic growth led to a search for alternative approaches that were more people- and community-centred.

The 1980s brought further disappointments as the economies of many countries in Africa and Latin America went into precipitous decline and were forced into budgetary cuts and readjustment. Indeed, for many parts of the world the 1980s have been labelled a 'lost decade'—though in the case of children the 1980s can also legitimately be described as the decade in which their cause was re-found.

The rediscovery of children as a group in their own right was prompted from two directions simultaneously. The first was the child survival revolution, which was later expanded to child survival and development. In 1982, under the energetic leadership of Executive Director James P. Grant, UNICEF launched an initiative to reduce preventable child deaths from conditions such as diarrhoea and measles, which in the late 20th century ought not to be life-threatening. Indeed, some 15 million children under the age of five were still dying every year, two thirds of them from readily preventable causes. James Grant called this the "silent emergency" that deserved worldwide action. This initiative found an extraordinary degree of global resonance and helped reactivate the people-centred development agenda and increase its political appeal.

The high-water mark of the child survival and development revolution was the 1990 World Summit for Children, at the time the largest-ever gathering of Heads of State and Government—including 71 Presidents and Prime Ministers. In all, the representatives of 159 governments committed themselves to a joint Declaration and Plan of Action on behalf of the world's children. For the first time, the global community agreed upon international goals—at the highest political level—to reduce rates of mortality and disease, malnutrition and illiteracy, and to reach specific targets by the year 2000.

The second factor propelling forward the children's cause was a regenerated campaign for child rights. This campaign had its genesis during and after World War I, when the right of children to special protection was first internationally acknowledged. In 1924, the League of Nations had adopted a World Child Welfare Charter. And later, after

In 1946, UNICEF distributed blankets and other forms of relief to children like this one in Greece.

SUB-SAHARAN AFRICA

▶ Progress for children in Africa has been slower and more uneven than in other regions.

▶ Risk of dying before age five is still higher than in any other region despite the decline in U5MR from 25 per cent in 1960 to 18 per cent in 1993. In recent years, it appears to have increased in several countries, including Madagascar, Zambia and Zimbabwe.

▶ Life expectancy, which increased from 37 to 51 years between 1950 and 1990, remains the lowest in the world.

▶ In the early 1980s, only 20 per cent of children in the region were immunized; in the early 1990s, about half were.

▶ The number of children in primary school has quadrupled since 1960. The girls' enrolment ratio more than doubled from 18 to 46 per cent between 1960 and 1990. Nevertheless, only half of eligible children are enrolled in primary school, and the gender gap remains wide.

▶ During the 1980s, the enrolment rate decreased in about half the region's countries. No other region has ever experienced such a set-back.

▶ Malnutrition has not declined, and one third of children suffer from stunting.

▶ On average, the number of children per mother has barely declined in 40 years: it is still more than 6, the highest of all regions.

World War II, non-governmental organizations (NGOs) lobbied the newly formed United Nations to endorse this document. As a result, in 1959, the UN General Assembly passed a new version of the Child Welfare Charter in the form of a Declaration of the Rights of the Child.

During the following two decades, however, the cause of children was progressively drowned out by the noise from so many others—the environment, for example, and world hunger. Accordingly, in an effort to bring children back to the public's attention, the NGO children's lobby pressed the UN to declare 1979 the International Year of the Child (IYC).

Rather than presenting development as the main context for addressing children's needs, IYC focused instead simply on the child. This was not a reversion to the previous welfarist approach since it involved airing many difficult issues in uncompromising terms that went beyond welfare and philanthropy—taking the wraps off such sensitive subjects as child labour, child abuse and child prostitution. IYC was also to pave the way for a major new advance for child rights—the replacement of the 1959 Declaration of the Rights of the Child with a more weighty international legal instrument.

In 1989, the UN General Assembly passed the Convention on the Rights of the Child. This entered into force in the following year, and as with the child survival and development revolution, it touched a highly responsive chord, and faced fewer obstacles to ratification than most other human rights instruments.

The year 1990 was, therefore, a watershed for children. The World Summit and the passage into international law of the Convention on the Rights of the Child were crowning moments of twin campaigns: for children at the leading edge of hu-

man development, and for children at the cutting edge of human rights.

These campaigns may have crystallized during the 1980s, but their expansion belongs to the whole course of the post-World War II and post-colonial period. In the decade of the 1990s, these campaigns have converged and begun to take on each other's colouring and perspective.

In the uncertainties of the post-cold war era, the outstanding question for UNICEF and other champions of the children's cause is whether the momentum for children will continue to grow. Amid the clamour generated by such issues as environmental sustainability, gender equality, debt forgiveness and ethnic self-determination, children may turn out to be just another concern whose moment in the sun is swiftly eclipsed. Alternatively, the new priority for 'child survival and development' and 'child rights' may actually echo a profound shift of human values and behaviour.

The following historical review commemorates UNICEF's 50th anniversary year and traces decade by decade how the cause of children internationally has evolved over the past 50 years. It explores the contribution of UNICEF against the backcloth of changing ideas in social and economic affairs, and tries to see where the children's cause is headed for the year 2000 and beyond.

The 1950s: Era of the mass disease campaign

The inclusion in UNICEF's founding resolution of the phrase "for child health purposes generally" opened the way for UNICEF to become a permanent fixture in the UN system. And it also paved the way for UNICEF involvement not only in child feeding but in public health.

During World War II and its

aftermath, disease rates had soared among weakened populations. In particular, forms of tuberculosis—the 'white plague'—had reached epidemic proportions. In Poland, for example, the child death rate from TB had multiplied four times during the war.

As a result, in 1947 the Scandinavian Red Cross societies sought assistance from UNICEF for an international tuberculosis campaign that aimed to immunize all uninfected European children. This was to be both the largest vaccination campaign ever undertaken and also the first one to use the BCG vaccine outside the controlled circumstances of the clinic.

There were some qualms that UNICEF would be treading on the territory of the fledgling World Health Organization (WHO), but it was argued that UNICEF would complement WHO's technical advisory role since it could offer material support in terms of vaccines, syringes and vehicles.

The international TB campaign set the tone for UNICEF's involvement in health care beyond emergency child feeding. Indeed, as the 1940s gave way to the 1950s, the predominant motif in international public health campaigns generally was the struggle to control or eradicate epidemic disease. These campaigns were among the first, and certainly the most spectacular, extensions of non-war-related international assistance. And they moved far beyond Europe, to Africa, Asia and Latin America. They also changed UNICEF's priorities—extending its programme geographically to countries in the Middle East, the Indian subcontinent and the Far East, as well as shifting its focus from emergency first aid for children to long-term preventive health care.

This attack on ill health was prompted both by demand and

supply. The demand came from the heavy case-load of infectious disease to be found among populations in the poverty-stricken 'underdeveloped' world. The supply came from the breakthroughs in medical technology of the previous half-century. New drugs and vaccines were becoming ever cheaper and, for the first time in history, offered a genuine prospect that age-old scourges could be swept away without waiting for the spread of doctors, hospitals and health centres. Used on a mass scale, and following a systematic geographical plan and timetable, the new techniques could—theoretically—force a specific disease to relinquish its hold over a whole population.

The disease that succumbed earliest and most dramatically to the mass campaign was yaws. This painful condition, spread by a micro-organism, could lead to total disability. It was found in tropical, poor and remote rural areas and was contracted through broken skin. In the early 1950s, there were thought to be around 20 million cases worldwide, over half of which were in Asia. The invention of penicillin transformed the prospects of cure. One shot cleared the ugly pink lesions, and a few more cleared the disease from the body.

The campaign against yaws with which UNICEF was most closely involved was in Indonesia. Mobile teams of lay health workers located the cases, and health professionals treated them. By 1955, these teams were treating over 100,000 yaws cases a month. Similarly in Thailand, nearly 1 million cases had been cured, and full eradication in Asia was becoming a distinct possibility.

The almost miraculous effect of the yaws cure also acted as a spur to other campaigns. One was tuberculosis: by the mid-1950s, 3.5 million children worldwide were being

As drugs and vaccines became cheaper in the 1950s, international public health campaigns began to focus on controlling epidemic disease through immunization.

tested for TB every month and over 1 million vaccinated. Trachoma too was under attack. This eye infection, which then affected up to 400 million people worldwide, was treated on a mass scale with an antibiotic ointment. Malaria was another priority. At the mid-point of the century, this disease had the highest incidence in the world— 200 million victims annually. The malarial frontier was rolled back by DDT spraying of people's homes.

Finally, leprosy sufferers could be offered a reprieve. As the first effective treatments for this stigmatizing condition came into use, they too were incorporated into the disease campaign machinery.

This enthusiasm for dealing with disease through technical interventions even extended to malnutrition. When in the early 1950s investigations among children on the African continent revealed widespread malnutrition, international public health experts were so attuned to the heroics of disease conquest that they behaved as if malnutrition, too, was an epidemic infection. They gave it medical labels—kwashiorkor and marasmus—and the medicine they prescribed was protein.

One of the most convenient forms of protein was milk. The alchemy that this particular blend of animal fat and protein could perform on child health was almost as sacrosanct a principle of nurture as motherhood. UNICEF was still heavily engaged with child feeding, and for the first two decades of its existence the heart of its efforts on behalf of child nutrition was the provision of milk.

This was greatly assisted by a reliable supply. In the early 1950s, the US had accumulated a vast reservoir of skim milk which, due to advances in dairy production, could be dried, preserved and later reconstituted. In 1954, the US Congress passed Public Law 480, through which the US offered aid organizations surplus farm produce free of charge. UNICEF was an important recipient; in 1957, it used this as part of its programme to provide milk via schools and health facilities to 4.5 million children and to pregnant and nursing mothers. In some countries, UNICEF also supported tropical dairying. In time, however, it was to replace milk-based interventions with sustainable solutions such as home-grown vegetables, fruits and poultry.

The mass disease campaigns certainly succeeded in reducing the levels of infection for both children and adults: in Ceylon, for example, between 1945 and 1960 the death rate from malaria dropped from 1,300 per million to zero. In fact, so successful were the campaigns that during the next decade they were blamed for igniting a population explosion. But, as experience was beginning to show, not everything about the campaigns was quite as perfect as their public image suggested.

The campaigns had been conceived as interim solutions—a means of holding some forms of ill health at bay until such time as regular health services could be set up. However, it was precisely this lack of a health support network that made the operation very difficult and expensive to mount and sustain. In places where trained health professionals were few, administration weak, communications poor and transport intermittent, the sharp and decisive stroke the disease campaign was meant to deliver could dissolve into a long, repetitive and inconclusive enterprise.

The campaign managers had underestimated the operational difficulties and the human complexities. In the 1950s and 1960s, contemporary adulation for technology and the 'quick fix' encouraged the enthusiasts of international public

ICEF-3898/Ling

Indonesia mounted the world's largest campaign against yaws—curable through penicillin—in the 1950s, employing large numbers of mobile male nurses working in the field.

health to believe that, with enough resources, better epidemiological surveillance and extra strategic refinements, they would finally reach their goal. Like their counterparts in other disciplines, the public health specialists were new to the challenges of development. They were bound to make mistakes.

For diseases like yaws, when people found painful sores disappearing as if by magic, they were happy to cooperate. And there were other notable successes, of which the greatest was the eventual eradication of smallpox. But for other diseases, people could not always see the cure work so directly and were therefore less likely to change their behaviour. One of the most difficult challenges was malaria.

The massive malaria campaign launched in 1955 by WHO and UNICEF finally failed because its chief architects misjudged the willingness of both humans and malarial mosquitoes to live, eat, sleep and generally behave according to technical assumptions. Eventually, the malaria warriors were forced to accept that without a basic service to back up and consolidate their gains, it was almost impossible to 'impose' health on a population unless it was geographically circumscribed—as, for example, in a relief camp.

The most important lesson to be learned from the programmes of the 1950s was that the people of Africa, Asia and Latin America were not a blank sheet of paper on which experts from the industrialized world could write their own version of progress. However, another decade at least was to pass before this lesson was fully absorbed.

The 1960s: Decade of development

In January 1961, the United Nations resolved that the decade of the 1960s would be the Decade of Development. President Kennedy launched the Decade at the UN in New York. Earlier, in his inaugural address as President, he had signalled a new sense of purpose in international affairs. He declared: "To those peoples in the huts and villages of half the globe struggling to break the bonds of mass misery, we pledge our best efforts to help them help themselves."

The rapidly decolonizing world thus embarked on a new age of partnership. In this view, to have one part of humanity live well while the other lived in penury was morally unacceptable. But there were also strategic considerations. In the ideological confrontation between East and West, the promise of poverty alleviation was a weapon to be deployed in the building of alliances.

As new countries rushed to freedom—no fewer than 17 former colonies in Africa achieved independence in 1960—the climate was one of excitement and hope. The new links being forged within the community of nations seemed to open up a new era of international peace and prosperity. The countries of the 'third world', having cast off their colonial status, now also needed to cast off their poverty. But for this they needed aid in the form of funds and know-how from their richer neighbours. Thus was born the push for development, a concept which along with more conventional notions of economic investment also embraced a degree of moral and humanitarian fervour.

During the late 1950s, the United Nations had begun to adapt its institutions to take on the development challenge. It already had technical expertise within its specialized agencies but it also needed a mechanism to channel financial resources. In 1957, therefore, it established a Special Fund to support the growth of infrastructure and industrialization. This was later to

MIDDLE EAST AND NORTH AFRICA

▶ This region has reduced child mortality faster than any other in the developing world. In 1960, one quarter of all children died before age five; by 1993, U5MR had been cut to 7 per cent. Nevertheless, the survival prospects of children are lower than those in regions where income is comparable.

▶ Immunization campaigns doubled coverage against the six main vaccine-preventable diseases, from 42 per cent in the early 1980s to 84 per cent a decade later. Iran, Jordan, Kuwait, Oman and Tunisia now report immunization rates of over 95 per cent.

▶ Total enrolment in primary schools more than doubled between 1970 and 1990. The girls' enrolment rate of 28 per cent in 1960 had soared by 1990 to 70 per cent.

▶ The female literacy rate more than doubled between 1970 and 1990. But two thirds of the region's estimated 65 million illiterate adults are women.

▶ Children fare differently depending on country of origin, residence and gender. The Sudan and Yemen have much higher child mortality rates than Kuwait and the United Arab Emirates. In Egypt and Tunisia, rural children are twice as likely to be malnourished as those in urban areas.

SOUTH ASIA

▶ One quarter of all the children in the world live in South Asia. In spite of lingering poverty, their survival prospects have improved considerably over the past three decades: in 1960, 1 in 4 children died by age five; by 1993, the number was 1 in 8.

▶ Life expectancy at birth rose from 39 to 60 years between 1950 and 1990, but women do not significantly outlive men, as they do in all other regions.

▶ The girls' net primary school enrolment ratio increased from 29 per cent in 1960 to 62 per cent in 1990. But the gender gap in education remains wide: a girl is 20 per cent less likely to attend primary school than a boy. Child labour is a major obstacle to education.

▶ By the early 1980s, 28 per cent of children were immunized against vaccine-preventable diseases; by the early 1990s, the immunization rate had almost tripled to 85 per cent. In Bangladesh, coverage soared from 1 to 74 per cent during the 1980s.

▶ Strong disparities persist. A child born in Sri Lanka can expect to live 72 years, one born in Bhutan 50 years.

▶ Malnutrition affects 60 per cent of children, by far the highest rate of any region.

be transformed into the United Nations Development Programme (UNDP).

At first blush, UNICEF with its modest humanitarian programme did not appear to belong to the new 'development' club. But no organization in the UN community could remain immune to the new currents of thinking. During the early 1960s, UNICEF tried to absorb the torrent of ideas and chart its own path within them. This quest was essentially guided by Dick Heyward, UNICEF's senior Deputy Executive Director and intellectual powerhouse from 1949 to 1981. In the process, UNICEF underwent the third important transformation in its history.

The turning-point was a special survey into the needs of children. This survey, initiated by UNICEF in 1960, took a year to complete, and was accompanied by 'state of the art' reports from the specialized agencies. These included: WHO, for the health needs of children; the Food and Agriculture Organization (FAO) and WHO, for the nutritional needs of children; the United Nations Educational, Scientific and Cultural Organization (UNESCO), for the educational needs of children; the UN Bureau of Social Affairs, for the social welfare needs of children; and the International Labour Organisation (ILO), for the work and livelihood needs of children. The final report, *Children of the Developing Countries*, represented a watershed in nations' outlook on how to help their most vulnerable citizens.

The report interwove social and economic strands concerning children's well-being in a fresh and innovative way and presented a theory of development that underlined the importance of satisfying human needs during various phases of childhood and pre-adulthood. In particular, it argued that children's

needs should be built into national development plans. Children should not be treated as if they were the orphans of the development process or merely its accidental baggage; they should be a focus of all policies directed at building up a country's 'human capital'. Just as over the course of the 20th century, the motto 'children first' had gained currency during times of war and sudden catastrophe, so a new version of the same motto had been articulated in the context of development.

This had major implications for the programmes UNICEF supported. They could no longer be confined to those run by subdepartments of Ministries of Health and Social Welfare. If children were a country's most precious resource, then their interests were not merely something to be addressed at times of distress. Rather, their well-being should be a specific target of investment and indeed of the whole development effort. The situation of children would have to be discussed within Ministries of National Planning, no less. And because children's concerns would have to be contemplated by research institutes and within national surveying and planning exercises, these were all activities that UNICEF would henceforth be willing to support. The importance UNICEF attached to 'planning for children' was confirmed in its special 1962 declaration of policy for the Development Decade, endorsed that year by the UN General Assembly.

The other major change was to abandon the compartmentalization of children's needs. In the future, UNICEF would consider the needs of children along with those of their parents and nurturers, and would take into account the 'whole' child. Instead of treating the child as a set of parts of which the only ones of concern were those related to physical well-being, UNICEF should be willing to address the child's broader intellectual and psychosocial needs. The immediate outcome was a change of policy whereby UNICEF for the first time—and to the satisfaction of the countries of the developing world—was willing to provide funds for formal and non-formal education.

Like many other members of the international humanitarian community, UNICEF set out over the next few years to show that the fields in which it was engaged lay at the heart of development. These were traditional arenas such as food and nutrition, and maternal and child health care. But they also included new ones such as education, women's issues, water supplies and sanitation. In these areas, UNICEF could provide material assistance in the form of equipment, drugs, vehicles and training stipends. In very poor environments, technical advice was futile without the wherewithal to put it into effect.

Because the humanitarian organizations were essentially field oriented, they learned this lesson faster than most. Other agencies focusing more on economic development had been relying largely on the formula of technical advice and cheap credit. This was a woefully inadequate response to poverty and its complex web of political, social, cultural and economic dimensions.

The humanitarian agencies, on the other hand, wanted ordinary families to receive tangible benefits. They were not interested in theoretical models derived from Western norms, only in trying to make things happen on the ground. Their vision of development was one in which pride of place went to the needs of the poor—and in the case of UNICEF, the needs of poor children.

But by the middle years of the decade one further consideration was looming over the horizon. The

demographers had discovered that recent declines in the death rate unaccompanied by matching declines in the birth rate were playing havoc with developing countries' population profiles. The kind of increase that had taken three centuries to happen in Europe was taking place in parts of Africa, Asia and Latin America within 50 to 75 years.

The resulting 'population explosion' threatened to undermine all the hard-won gains of human progress and subject the planet's non-renewable resources to overwhelming strain. It quickly became an international *cause célèbre* that all agents of development were forced to address. The technological instrument was readily available—artificial contraception.

But at a meeting in Addis Ababa in 1966, the UNICEF Executive Board opted for the concept of 'responsible parenthood', whose primary objective was to improve the survival, well-being and quality of life of the child, the mother and the family. It did not mean that family planning was eschewed; it simply meant that family planning was seen in the broader context of maternal and child health, embracing improvements in the status of women (a harbinger of the conferences in Cairo and Beijing), promoting literacy, raising the age of marriage and avoiding unwanted pregnancies.

In 1965, UNICEF was awarded the Nobel Peace Prize. Earlier that year, Maurice Pate, who had led the organization since its inception, died. His place as Executive Director was taken by Henry Labouisse. Under his careful statesmanship the UN's organization for children became gradually more prominent in the issues of the day. Even so, it was not until 1972 that the UN formally recognized that UNICEF was a development, rather than a welfare, organization and began to review its

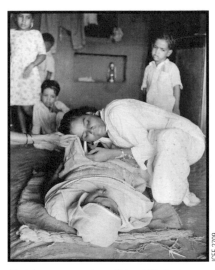

Training a country's traditional birth attendants in pre- and postnatal care and safe delivery techniques was a strategy to reduce maternal mortality rates and protect newborns.

Village water supplies

UNICEF/5894/Lemoyne

In the summer of 1967, a chronic drought and an alarming drop in India's underground water reserves ignited a revolution in village water supplies—and started a process of improvement whose effects are felt to this day throughout Africa, Asia and Latin America.

Around 70 per cent of India is separated from the water table by a deep rock shield, and many Indian villages that rely on underground water are extremely vulnerable to drought. In the 1950s, the Indian Government had identified 153,000 villages as 'water-scarce'—most of them in hard-rock areas.

In the 1960s, there was a series of droughts, and in the summer of 1967 the situation became critical in Bihar and Uttar Pradesh when many of the existing wells dried up. It would have taken many weeks for the villagers to sink more wells using traditional methods, and some 250 villages were faced with evacuation to refugee camps. UNICEF flew in 11 pneumatic drilling rigs capable of boring through 150 feet of rock in about eight hours. When this emergency had passed, the rigs were transferred for use in drought emergencies elsewhere.

As the water table continued to recede, the Government asked UNICEF for more drilling equipment. Between 1970 and 1974, UNICEF shipped in 125 hammer rigs, along with trucks and spare parts. Each of these rigs could drill about 100 boreholes a year—theoretically supplying water to 12,000 villages and about 9 million people.

But boreholes also need efficient pumps. Most of the handpumps in India at that time were poor-quality cast-iron replicas of European and American models that had usually been designed for family use. But while pumps in the US might have been used by a farming family three or four times a day, those in India were used incessantly, with women and children queuing up to use each pump from dawn till dusk. Not surprisingly, the pumps frequently broke down. When UNICEF did a survey of boreholes and pumps in two states, it found that 75 per cent of the pumps were out of action.

Clearly, India needed a more rugged pump. A 1975 workshop sponsored by UNICEF, the World Health Organization (WHO), the Government of India and the government of Karnataka state summed it up: a design simple enough to be manufactured in unsophisticated workshops, easy to maintain and costing no more than US$200.

Rather than start from scratch, however, UNICEF water supply staff searched for the most durable pump then available. They settled on the Sholapur pump that had originally been designed by a self-taught Indian mechanic. They modified this for easier mass production and maintenance, renamed it the India Mark II and field-tested it in 1976 and 1977.

Mass production of the India Mark II started in 1977-1978, with 600 units a month. By 1984, 36 manufacturers were producing 100,000 pumps a year. By 1987, annual production had reached 200,000. With exports to other countries in Asia, as well as to Africa and Latin America, the India Mark II was well on its way to becoming the best-known deep-well handpump in the world. Meanwhile, development has continued—and has produced the more user-friendly India Mark III.

In less than two decades, more than 1 million of the pumps have been produced, and they have proved both reliable and durable. A 1984 survey, commissioned by UNICEF, found that in six states in India, 80 per cent were operational at any one time. Every year about 50,000 new pumps are installed in India, and an equal number are finding their way into communities throughout the developing world.

Photo: Safe water, a primary requisite for health, is also a delight.

work under its economic and social, rather than humanitarian, machinery. And it was not until later still that the idea of investing in children would move away from the notion of philanthropy and into the development mainstream.

The 1970s: Era of alternatives

By the early 1970s, the development movement was running out of steam. The idea that transfers of capital and technical know-how would quickly dispense with gross poverty had proved misconceived. During the previous decade, many developing countries had achieved high rates of economic growth—increases of 5 per cent or more in GNP—but little of this had 'trickled down' to the poor. On the contrary, their numbers had swollen—as had the gap between rich and poor people, and between rich and poor nations. The rates of population growth were partly to blame; but equally important were policies based on simplistic assumptions. This much had become clearer to the growing community of development analysts attached to universities, governments and international organizations. They busily began to diagnose what had gone wrong and set out on the quest for alternatives.

This led to a new climate of development thinking. Since economic growth did not automatically sweep poverty away, development analysts decided that the second Development Decade must also include measures deliberately targeted at the poor—to help them meet their basic needs for food, water, housing, health and education.

In the past, economists and planners had looked upon these rather as forms of 'consumption' unconnected to economic productivity. Now their thinking began to change. In 1972, Robert McNamara, then President of the World Bank, made what was seen as a landmark statement. Governments in developing countries, he said, should redesign their policies so as to meet the needs of the poorest 40 per cent of their people—and relieve their poverty directly. The cornerstone of the new development strategy was thus an explicit attack on poverty—albeit one so mounted as not to damage economic prospects. Its economic slogans were: 'redistribution with growth', and 'meeting basic needs'.

As policy makers began to focus less on economies and more on people, they realized that those bit-players, the humanitarians, had actually met the new criteria for success rather well. While the economic planners had focused on dams and factories, the humanitarians had focused on the village, the community, the family and the individual. They appeared to be putting into effect British economist E. F. Schumacher's concept that 'small is beautiful'—a proposition that seemed to encapsulate the spirit of the era. NGOs, with their localized mini-projects, already enjoyed an intimate relationship with the poor; UNICEF had similar advantages. Although it worked at one stage removed, its connections with communities were certainly much closer than those of any other player in the UN hierarchy. Within the development club, the programmes supported by the humanitarians, including UNICEF, began to enjoy a new legitimacy.

The early 1970s saw two events of particular significance for international development. One was the OPEC oil shock, which sent prices soaring and ended the era of cheap energy and cheap industrialization—and therefore of cheap development. The other was the global food shortage brought about by two disastrous world harvests in 1972 and 1974. The UN responded to the

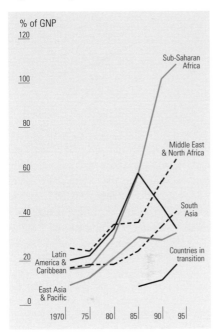

Fig. 6 Rising debt

Total debt as a percentage of GNP increased in all regions over the period 1971-1993. Latin America's high debt levels of the 1980s have since fallen. Sub-Saharan Africa's debt, which has continued to soar, now surpasses its GNP.

Source: World Bank, *World debt tables 1994-95, volume 2*, Washington, D.C., 1994.

Note: Data for sub-Saharan Africa excludes South Africa.

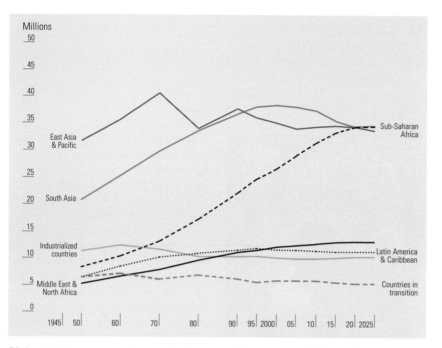

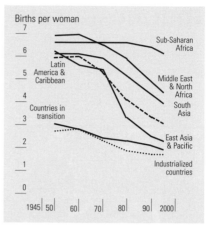

The **total fertility rate** (average number of births per woman) in sub-Saharan Africa has recently started to fall, which should stabilize the number of births in the future. All other regions show large reductions in their fertility rates. In East Asia and the Pacific, the 1995 fertility rate is little more than a third of the 1950 level.

Births are projected to level off in all regions by the year 2000, except for sub-Saharan Africa, where the continuing increase in population will result in the annual number of births reaching 35 million by 2025.

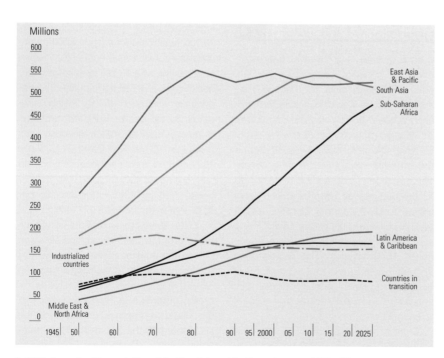

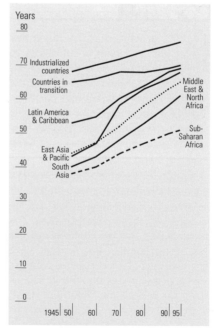

In 1975, the **under-16 population** of the East Asia and Pacific region topped 500 million, and stabilized at that level. South Asia is projected to reach that level by the year 2000, and sub-Saharan Africa by 2025.

Source for four figures: United Nations, *World population prospects—the 1994 revision*, New York, 1995.

Life expectancy increased by 10 years or more in most regions between 1950 and 1995, with South Asia and East Asia and the Pacific showing gains of 20 years or more.

In 1976, the UNICEF Executive Board committed itself to the basic services approach. By this time, UNICEF and WHO were already well on the way to agreeing on an alternative approach to health care. They had seen that health care structures in developing countries had evolved mainly into pale facsimiles of the high-tech delivery systems familiar in the industrialized world. Given the lack of resources, this had distorted priorities and led to a disregard of the basic principles of public health. Up to 90 per cent of a developing country's health budget could be absorbed by a handful of city hospitals serving the élite, while out in the countryside villagers were obliged to walk miles to the most rudimentary dispensary. The poor might occasionally receive visits from mobile teams of smallpox eradicators or water engineers, but services they urgently needed—notably those for maternal and child health—were rarely available.

At a time when heart transplants and *in vitro* fertilization were stunning the world, millions of people—up to three quarters of the population in many countries—remained beyond the reach of modern health care. Moreover, the sicknesses that afflicted them, or more usually their children, were simple and obvious. The poor were suffering and dying from diarrhoea, fevers and respiratory infections that no longer constituted a threat in the industrialized world and indeed were viewed there in the most pedestrian terms. They were the diseases of poverty. And they were disrupting, and in some cases destroying, the lives of hundreds of millions of children and families.

In 1978, at an international conference in Alma Ata in the then USSR, Ministers of Health from all over the developing world agreed that their health delivery systems must be radically restructured to provide 'primary health care' (PHC) for all their citizens. The critical service was care for mothers and children before, during and after birth. Added to this were emergency first aid, surveillance of young child growth, disease control, family planning, safe water supplies and environmental sanitation. As with basic services, ordinary people would be enlisted in their own preventive care. This radical vision set an ambitious goal, 'Health for All by the Year 2000'.

During the first two Development Decades, UNICEF had argued that working for children was part of a much larger social and economic movement. But this emphasis on development and on other great issues of the day had a drawback. It meant that, even within the humanitarian community, the special needs of childhood and of disadvantaged child groups were in danger of being submerged. Anxious to project children back into the limelight, the Geneva-based International Union for Child Welfare and other child-related NGOs managed to persuade the UN to declare 1979 the International Year of the Child. Initially reluctant to commit its energies to a celebratory and possibly superficial affair, UNICEF was eventually persuaded to play a leading role. IYC proved far from superficial. It was a remarkable success. The children's cause had reached another turning-point.

The 1980s: Campaign for child survival

As the 1980s—the third Development Decade—dawned, the countries of the developing world were beginning to feel the chill of global recession. In the industrialized countries, growth had slumped and unemployment had risen to levels higher than at any time since the

ORS: The medical advance of the century

UNICEF/5884/Lemoyne

During the 1980s, UNICEF launched the 'child survival and development revolution', concentrating its efforts on four potent methods of saving children's lives—growth monitoring, breastfeeding, immunization, and the use of oral rehydration salts (ORS)—the best way of combating the dehydration caused by diarrhoea.

The British medical journal *The Lancet* has described ORS as "potentially the most important medical advance of this century."

In the late 1970s, acute diarrhoea was killing around 5 million children each year. The obvious response to dehydration—giving the child water to drink—did not work because the liquid rushed through the digestive tract too quickly to be absorbed by the body tissues. The only answer seemed to be to bypass the digestive system altogether and rehydrate the body using an intravenous drip. This is an invasive and traumatic procedure for a child. And because it must be administered by someone with medical training, it is

completely impractical for most episodes of childhood diarrhoea, which take place out of range of any kind of medical attention.

In 1968, researchers in Bangladesh and India discovered that adding glucose to water and salt in the right proportions enabled the liquid to be absorbed through the intestinal wall. So anyone suffering from diarrhoea could replace the lost fluids and salts simply by drinking this solution.

One of the first large-scale field applications of oral rehydration salts took place in 1971 during the Bangladesh war of independence when outbreaks of cholera swept through refugee camps. Of the 3,700 victims treated with ORS, over 96 per cent survived.

Home-made versions of ORS are not difficult to make and can help prevent diarrhoeal dehydration. The Bangladesh Rural Advancement Committee (BRAC), for example, has shown mothers in Bangladesh how to mix water, salt and molasses to prevent dehydration when a

child falls ill with diarrhoea. Families can also use the rice water from the cooking pot to prevent dehydration. ORS, however, is best to treat dehydration when it occurs, as well as to prevent it.

ORS sachets are now being produced, with UNICEF support, in 60 developing countries. Total production is around 500 million sachets a year—costing around 10 cents (US) each.

Around half of all diarrhoea cases in the world's poorest countries are now treated with oral rehydration therapy (ORT), which means that ORS as well as recommended home fluids are given. This is a vast improvement over the 1 per cent level of usage at the beginning of the 1980s. But there is still an urgent need to make ORT more accessible.

One of the problems is that the medical establishment is still reluctant to accept ORS. In the United States, for example, it costs almost 10 times as much to treat dehydration with an intravenous drip in a hospital as it does to administer ORS, yet the intravenous method prevails. Drug companies, too, stand to gain more by selling antidiarrhoeal drugs, most of which are useless and some of which are dangerous.

Around 8,000 children still die each day from diarrhoeal dehydration, a toll the world can and must reduce with ORT.

Photo: A Cambodian mother feeds oral rehydration salts to her dehydrated child.

1930s. This slow-down was transmitted to the developing countries, and one major consequence was an international debt crisis—sparked off in 1982 when Mexico suspended interest payments on an accumulating mountain of debt. As a result, many African and Latin American countries were hit by recession and directives that they structurally adjust their economies. The situation had severe implications for the poor, in time prompting a call similar to that of the 'emergency for children' in the 1970s: 'adjustment with a human face'. The concept responded so persuasively to the anxiety about what was happening to vulnerable groups in developing countries that it quickly entered the lexicon of international development. In a very real sense, it served to take UNICEF into the mainstream of economic and social policy-making, giving UNICEF a voice and credibility not experienced before in these circles.

At the same time, there were emerging signs of hope for the children's cause. The evolution of the 'basic services' and PHC approaches had given the practitioners of social and human development a new sense of purpose. And the success of the 1979 International Year of the Child implied that the time was ripe for a new push on behalf of children. UNICEF's new Executive Director, James P. Grant, was determined to capitalize on these opportunities.

In December 1982, in his annual *State of the World's Children* report, James Grant launched an initiative known as the child survival revolution, later including child development. This campaign reversed conventional wisdom. Rates of infant and young child mortality had previously been seen as measurements of a country's development. Now UNICEF suggested a direct attack on infant and child mortality as

an instrument of development.

In a throw-back to the great disease campaigns of the 1950s, UNICEF now proposed to vanquish common infections of early childhood using simple medical technologies. From the primary health care package, it singled out four techniques, which collectively were referred to as 'GOBI': 'G' for growth monitoring to keep a regular check on child well-being; 'O' for oral rehydration therapy to treat bouts of childhood diarrhoea; 'B' for breastfeeding as the perfect nutritional start in life; and 'I' for immunization against the six vaccine-preventable childhood killers: tuberculosis, diphtheria, whooping cough, tetanus, polio and measles. One of the strengths of this prescription was that all the techniques were low cost.

Initially, some members of the international public health community had reservations about the 'child survival and development revolution'. They were concerned about its narrow emphasis on a few primary health care ingredients. But the cause of child survival found an extraordinary degree of worldwide resonance, gathering a wide range of allies—national, international, bilateral, non-governmental—and from all walks of public and professional life.

This accumulation of popular and political support was not accidental. It was the result of a sophisticated use of communications, taking advantage of two fundamental developments over previous decades. First, there had been a dramatic expansion worldwide of basic education. Second, a media revolution had brought millions more people within reach of radio and television. Previous strategies had been hampered by the difficulty of 'imposing' health on unreceptive populations. But at this point, the new communications channels

Fig. 9 Under-5 mortality rate dropping

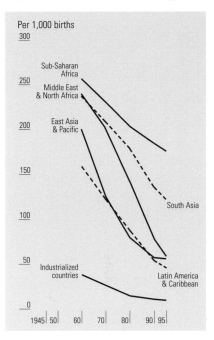

The under-5 mortality rate per 1,000 births has decreased in every region. In the Middle East and North Africa region, the rate is now only a quarter of what it was in 1960.

Fig. 10 Total under-5 deaths down

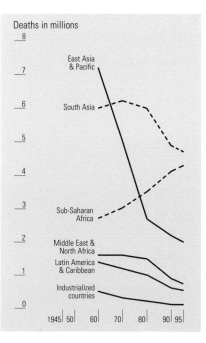

Under-5 deaths are declining everywhere except in sub-Saharan Africa, where a strong increase in births has meant a rise in total deaths.

Source for both figures: UNICEF.

59

Fig. 11 Measles immunization
high and holding

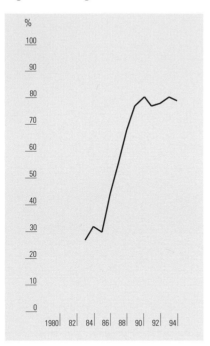

The percentage of the developing world's children under one who are protected against measles increased dramatically during the 1980s, and the coverage level achieved by 1990 is being maintained.

Source: WHO and UNICEF, September 1995.

opened up a different option—persuasion.

During the 1980s, UNICEF developed and fine-tuned a strategy of social mobilization. Not only did it enlist the media and advertising industries, it also invited partners from every nook and cranny of society—from religious leaders to Goodwill Ambassadors, from Heads of State to municipal mayors, from sports personalities to parliamentarians, from professional associations to trade unions—to join the child survival and development movement and spread its message.

At the international level, a Task Force for Child Survival and Development, including all the big-league players in international health—the Rockefeller Foundation, UNDP, UNICEF, the World Bank and WHO—was established to resolve technical issues associated with the campaign and help build its momentum. The campaign thus became far broader than UNICEF itself, which explains the use of the vivid phrase, 'a grand alliance for children'.

But whatever the power of the alliance, much of its success was still due to the extraordinary energy that James Grant injected into it personally and with which he infected others. His visits to scores of presidents and prime ministers did much to raise the visibility of the children's cause, and systematic lobbying within regional bodies such as the Association of South-East Asian Nations (ASEAN), the League of Arab States (LAS), the Organization of American States (OAS), the Organization of African Unity (OAU), the Organization of the Islamic Conference (OIC) and the South Asian Association for Regional Cooperation (SAARC) helped build political will.

In November 1985, at a special ceremony to commemorate the UN's 40th anniversary, nations recommitted themselves to the target originally set in 1977—universal child immunization (UCI) by 1990. Of the four GOBI elements, the expanded programme on immunization (EPI) had been taken up with the greatest enthusiasm in the largest number of countries, including the most populous on earth, China and India.

From an average at the beginning of the decade of 15 per cent immunization coverage, some developing countries had already pushed their rates to 60 per cent or more. A goal that a few years before seemed completely unattainable was now within striking distance.

During the rest of the 1980s, scores of developing countries conducted an all-out drive to reach a coverage of 80 per cent child immunization or more (75 per cent in Africa). This international effort, described as perhaps the greatest mobilization in peacetime history, succeeded in spite of the major cutbacks in social services necessitated by the economic recession and adjustment crisis.

Some voices were raised against the disproportionate share of public health resources used for childhood immunization. But the energy behind the campaign was such that in practice it spilled over into almost every area of maternal and child well-being—carrying in its wake a much wider range of primary health care services.

Towards the end of the decade, optimism was warranted on several fronts. Nutritional progress was encouraging enough to permit the World Summit to establish the goal of halving the 1990 rate of child malnutrition by the year 2000. Many countries in Latin America and the Caribbean and in Asia are improving child nutrition. Indeed, during the 1980s, nutritional status improved in every region of the world (only marginally in sub-Saharan

UNICEF and the stars

UNICEF/94-0468/Press

For most of its 50 years, UNICEF has benefited greatly from the support of internationally known personalities. Danny Kaye pioneered the role, as UNICEF's first Ambassador at large. For over three decades, beginning in 1953, he helped represent UNICEF and the needs of children in the international community. Audrey Hepburn also served as Goodwill Ambassador for UNICEF, from 1988 until her untimely death in January 1993. Her deeply sensitive appeals for children while visiting Ethiopia, Somalia and the Sudan cannot be forgotten.

UNICEF now has five Goodwill Ambassadors, personal representatives of the UNICEF Executive Director, volunteering their time and talents to draw the public's attention to the needs of children.

Current Ambassadors

▶ *Sir Peter Ustinov*—Goodwill Ambassador for over 25 years, he has won awards for his uniquely entertaining UNICEF public service announcements and for special documentaries on the situation of children in China and Russia. He represents UNICEF in numerous forums.

▶ *Liv Ullmann*—One of the first outsiders to visit refugee camps in Kampuchea in 1979, she also helped draw attention to a little-publicized famine in Ethiopia when she was photographed with children there in the mid-1980s. She continues her advocacy for children.

▶ *Tetsuko Kuroyanagi*—A well-known Japanese television personality, she has raised more than US$20 million in Japan through programmes about the UNICEF-supported projects she has visited.

▶ *Harry Belafonte*—A strong UNICEF voice for Africa in concert appearances and in special appeals, he has most recently advocated for the children of Rwanda.

▶ *Lord Attenborough*—Became familiar with UNICEF's work while making the films *Gandhi* in India and *Cry Freedom* in South Africa; both have been successful benefit fund-raisers for UNICEF.

In addition, a number of celebrated actors, artists, singers and sports figures donate their talents to advocate for children on behalf of UNICEF as **Special Representatives**, including:

▶ *Roger Moore*—A tireless advocate for children on many issues, he has become the major spokesperson for the Kiwanis-UNICEF initiative to eliminate iodine deficiency disorders (IDD).

▶ *Sir Edmund Hillary*—Has been giving special support to the salt iodization initiative to protect children from IDD in the Himalayas.

▶ *Vanessa Redgrave*—Has raised funds and public awareness for children in former Yugoslavia through a series of events in Bosnia and Herzegovina, and Croatia, as well as in London and New York.

▶ *Judy Collins*—Recently visited children in Viet Nam, has also been an envoy for peace in Bosnia and Herzegovina and Croatia, supporting the book *I dream of peace* on the wartime experiences of children. (See also page 15.)

▶ *Imran Khan*—Has used his international profile in cricket to support health and immunization programmes in Bangladesh, Pakistan, Sri Lanka and Thailand.

▶ *Johann Olav Koss*—The voice of UNICEF's Olympic Aid support programme for the 1996 Olympic Games in Atlanta.

▶ *Mario Kreutzberger*—Includes messages for UNICEF in his popular television programme 'Sabado Gigante', reaching a huge audience in Latin America and other Spanish-speaking countries.

Julio Iglesias, Leon Lai, Nana Mouskouri and *Youssou N'Dour* are other performers who have given generously of their time and talents in benefit concerts and appearances for UNICEF.

Photo: Harry Belafonte, who works tirelessly on behalf of children, visited Rwanda in 1994.

Africa), and in every category of malnutrition except anaemia.

Moreover, extraordinary improvements were made in access to safe drinking water. According to WHO's end-of-decade review, between 1981 and 1990, the proportions of families with access to safe drinking water rose from 38 to 66 per cent in South-East Asia, from 66 to 79 per cent in Latin America, and from 32 to 45 per cent in Africa.

In total, during the International Drinking Water Supply and Sanitation Decade (1981-1990), an additional 1.2 billion people gained access to safe water, and about 770 million to adequate sanitation. This has continued in the 1990s, so that by 1994, a further 780 million gained access to water.

By the end of the decade, the child survival and development revolution was estimated to have saved the lives of 12 million children. However, it was never aimed exclusively at saving children's lives and preventing childhood disease and disability. The wider purpose of the revolution was to revitalize the flagging cause of human-centred development and to place children at the leading edge.

One result was the international conference held in 1990 under the auspices of UNDP, UNESCO, UNICEF and the World Bank in Jomtien (Thailand), which set the target of 'Education for All by the Year 2000'. And in subsequent years, the World Bank tripled its lending for basic education to US$1 billion.

Also in 1990, UNDP brought out its first annual *Human Development Report*, which declared human beings to be both the means and the ends of development. Human, rather than economic, prospects were once again beginning to take pride of place.

The momentum behind human-centred development was particu-

larly sustained by the activities of women. International organizations such as UNICEF began to recognize that women had an importance that went beyond their biologically or socially determined maternal roles: that women were also economic providers, organizers and leaders. In many parts of the developing world, women made up one third of heads of households.

Thus far, the development process had pushed women to the margins. This not only excluded them from social and economic participation but it also acted as a powerful brake on development in general. Future progress would mean, therefore, that investment would have to be affirmatively structured in favour of women: that development would have to be 'gendered'.

This had major implications for UNICEF. Its child survival and development prescription did have two elements that directly supported the women's agenda—female education and birth spacing. But for the much more important GOBI ingredients, women were cast in an exclusively maternal role. Throughout the 1980s, UNICEF resisted becoming involved in the mainstream of the women's cause. Towards the end of the decade, however, it re-evaluated its policy on women in development to take on the language and dynamic of women's rights, with a special focus on girls.

The movement in the direction of women's rights also coincided with mounting pressure for the rights of children, which had hung fire somewhat in the years following the 1959 Declaration of the Rights of the Child but had been rekindled by IYC. The NGO community working on behalf of children took advantage of this renewed concern for children to argue that special protection for children should be more than a high-sounding principle; it

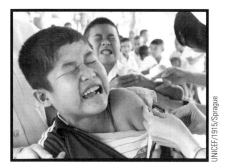

Global immunization reached an average 80 per cent of children in 1990, achieved through national campaigns, immunization days and other intensive efforts. Children were immunized at school in Thailand.

should also be enshrined in law.

Population growth and rapid rates of industrialization were putting increasing pressures on childhood and family life. The most conspicuous symptom of social stress and family breakdown was the increasing number of children working on city streets—with some also living there. In Latin America, where the phenomenon was at its most acute, there were thought to be several million street children.

Meanwhile, many other children were also being damaged by forces that went beyond the general rubric of poverty and underdevelopment. These included child victims of mass violence and warfare, and children with disabilities. They also included children suffering from exploitation—as workers and labourers, or as objects of commercial sexual gratification. In the mid-1980s, UNICEF coined a new term to cover all these categories of childhood disadvantage—children in especially difficult circumstances (CEDC).

At this point, UNICEF began to analyse CEDC situations and evolve policy responses. The international children's NGOs, on the other hand, were more concerned with advocacy and legislation to protect these children and bring their exploiters to book. After IYC, they had helped establish an intergovernmental group under the auspices of the UN Commission on Human Rights, which had begun to draft a convention to replace the 1959 Declaration of the Rights of the Child. The NGOs' input was critical to this process and helped to keep it moving.

In 1987, recognizing the potential convergence of the child survival and development revolution with the thrust for children's rights, UNICEF threw its weight into the child rights ring. Although its support arrived relatively late,

UNICEF's capacity for international mobilization was decisive.

In 1989, the UN General Assembly adopted the Convention on the Rights of the Child. On 2 September 1990, the Convention entered into force as international law. Within a year, more than 90 countries had ratified, and by end-September 1995 the total was 179. No human rights convention has ever attained such widespread ratification, nor so quickly.

Almost simultaneously, the campaign for child survival and development reached a peak. On 30 September 1990, 71 Heads of State or Government took their seats at a World Summit for Children. The climax of the occasion, held under the auspices of the UN in New York, was the joint signing of a World Declaration and 10-point Plan of Action comprising a set of child-related human development goals for the year 2000. These included targeted reductions in infant and maternal mortality, child malnutrition and illiteracy, as well as targeted levels of access to basic services for health and family planning, education, water and sanitation.

The Summit was one of the most important events in UNICEF's history: it marked the moment at which children's issues had reached such a high point on the international agenda that there seemed nowhere higher for them to go.

The immediate post-cold war period was a time of great optimism in international affairs. But it was also a time at which the wider development movement had reached a nadir. In the face of debt and structural adjustment, environmental degradation, the deepening crisis in Africa and the onset of AIDS, the 1980s had been labelled development's 'lost decade'. But for children, the 1980s was the decade in which their cause was not lost, but re-found.

LATIN AMERICA AND THE CARIBBEAN

▶ Over the past 50 years, children in Latin America have benefited from two major advantages compared to those in other regions: better educated parents, especially mothers, and a high degree of urbanization.

▶ The net primary enrolment ratio for girls increased from 57 per cent to 87 per cent between 1960 and 1990. Their secondary enrolment ratio is 49 per cent, the highest among the developing regions. The gender gap at both primary and secondary levels is very small.

▶ The mortality rate of children under age five was 15 per cent in 1960 and 5 per cent in 1993, the lowest in the developing world.

▶ In 1981, 45 per cent of children were immunized against vaccine-preventable diseases; in 1993, the rate of immunization had increased to 80 per cent. Polio was eliminated from the region in 1994.

▶ On average, a mother had 6 children in 1950; in 1990, the average was 3.

▶ Interregional differences remain stark. A Cuban can expect to live as long as a Dane, whereas a Peruvian's prospects are not much better than those of a person in Botswana. In Brazil, a poor child is five times more likely to die before the first birthday than a rich child; in Venezuela, a poor child is 10 times more likely to be malnourished than a rich one.

COUNTRIES IN TRANSITION

▶ During the three decades following World War II, Eastern Europe achieved almost universal access to basic social services for children. By the early 1970s, malnutrition and illiteracy were almost eradicated, the literacy rate and primary school enrolment ratio were above 90 per cent. In the early 1980s, the immunization rate was the highest of all regions.

▶ By the 1970s, social conditions had approached those in industrialized countries. Poor economic growth and widespread inefficiencies in the 1980s and turmoil following the political transition in the 1990s, however, have caused serious deterioration.

▶ Diphtheria, polio, respiratory illnesses and cholera are on the rise. The immunization rate has declined from 88 per cent in the mid-1980s to 77 per cent in the early 1990s.

▶ Since 1990, child mortality has increased in Albania, Russia and Ukraine. In other countries, easily treatable respiratory illnesses have again become the leading cause of infant mortality.

▶ In Russia and Ukraine, the life expectancy of men dropped by five years between 1989 and 1993 to a level actually lower than the official retirement age.

The 1990s: A decade for children's rights

Within three years of the World Summit for Children, 105 industrialized and developing countries, covering a total of 88 per cent of the world's children, had prepared national programmes of action (NPAs) for meeting the World Summit goals. In many cases, governments had used the process to bring together different sectors of society—governmental and non-governmental—in a joint endeavour. In some countries, Brazil and India for example, the same process also took place at state and even municipal levels.

The Summit had certainly been a star-studded and spectacular event. But it has not been allowed to vanish into the past as a one-off occurrence. Instead, it was used as a launching pad for a wider process of planning and commitment for children. In the 1960s, UNICEF had found it difficult to gain serious attention for such an idea. In the 1990s, however, Heads of State have given it their imprimatur, and made a strong commitment to the defence of children and reaching goals on their behalf—some world leaders even identifying these with their own personal political platforms.

Meanwhile, in a replay of the 1970s, the 1990s have become a decade in which the response of the UN system to the flagging development movement has been to embark on a series of global conferences. The UN Conference on Environment and Development (Rio de Janeiro, 1992) was followed by conferences on nutrition (Rome, 1992); human rights (Vienna, 1993); population and development (Cairo, 1994); social development (Copenhagen, March 1995); and women (Beijing, September 1995). Still to come is the 'City Summit' (Istanbul, June 1996). During the preparatory stages for all these conferences and at the meetings themselves, UNICEF has done its best to keep children's concerns prominently in view, actively promoting the social agenda encapsulated in the Declaration of the World Summit for Children.

In addition, a set of mid-decade goals for children has been established, starting with regional meetings in Africa and South Asia. In September 1993, on the third Summit anniversary, the United Nations Secretary-General convened a round table in New York called *Keeping the Promise to Children*, which reiterated the commitment to the Summit goals and endorsed mid-decade targets. These include universal ratification of the Convention on the Rights of the Child, and progress towards universal primary education, as well as targets for the control of specific diseases and nutritional deficiencies. By mid-decade, the aim was to have eradicated, or reduced by a specified amount, neonatal tetanus, malnutrition, polio, vitamin A deficiency, guinea worm disease and iodine deficiency disorders, as well as diarrhoeal and vaccine-preventable diseases (Panel 15).

The funding strategy for attaining these goals has been described as 'the 20/20 initiative': a call for developing countries to direct at least 20 per cent of their budgets to basic needs, and for industrialized countries to earmark 20 per cent of their development assistance for the same purpose. The 20/20 initiative has also gathered international support. In 1995 at the World Summit for Social Development in Copenhagen, UNDP, UNESCO, the United Nations Population Fund (UNFPA), UNICEF and WHO all backed it as a means of generating sufficient additional resources (US$30 billion-US$40 billion per

Making child rights constitutional in Brazil

UNICEF/1443/Edinger

In Brazil, for decades, there had been pressure from NGOs and children's organizations for protecting children battered by poverty and hunger and despised by sections of the community. The most vulnerable children were those living or working on the streets. Often subjected to violence and repression from the police and armed groups, they and their advocates mounted the call for reform. In 1985, they founded the National Street Children's Movement, which in 1986 held its first Congress in Brasilia.

Brazil had then just emerged from 21 years of authoritarian rule and was in the process of drafting a new democratic Constitution. It was a golden opportunity for children to enshrine their rights in law. Even so, it was a daunting task. UNICEF played an important role in strengthening and broadening the alliance of institutions working for children and provided technical support for the drafting process.

The campaign received a boost in 1986 when the Government established a National Committee on the Child and the Constitution. Along with representatives from government ministries, a wide variety of NGOs participated, including the National Street Children's Movement. UNICEF worked with the Committee in a number of ways: providing a secretariat and technical assistance, recruiting private sector support and helping widen the network of groups and organizations involved.

This momentum led to a widespread public campaign—including mass gatherings of children in a number of cities, as well as demonstrations in front of the National Congress. Organizations and NGOs from around the country proposed drafts for two constitutional amendments, which were endorsed by 200,000 voters and presented to the Constituent Assembly. These proposals ultimately became the chapter on the rights of children and adolescents in the Constitution—passed by a vote of 435 to 8.

The success of the Constitution was followed by an even greater victory two years later, when the *Statute of the Child*

and Adolescent was approved by both houses of the National Congress, legally obligating the Government to protect child rights. Children were involved in gaining its acceptance, with more than 5,000 meeting in Brasilia. João de Deus, one of the organizers, recalls, "The day the children occupied the Senate was the most important day of my life....There were congressmen crying who gave up their seats to the children."

The *Statute* defines children as citizens with clearly stated rights to respect, dignity and freedom. It also gives precedence to important needs in a child's life, such as health, education, sports and leisure. Special provisions guarantee children's protection as a matter of "absolute priority."

To ensure that the *Statute*'s provisions are enforced, Councils for the Rights of the Child and Adolescent were set up at federal, state and local levels, with members drawn from diverse backgrounds. These Councils have the authority to spend an allocated budget and to raise additional funds. This strengthens their work and helps provide protection for the most vulnerable children.

Upon this strong foundation, the Councils now face the challenge of continuing to transform and put into practice the nation's commitment towards its children as expressed in the Constitution.

Photo: Poverty forces vulnerable families on to the streets.

annum) to ensure that by the end of the century everyone would have access to basic social services. A number of national governments have endorsed these principles and committed themselves to move in the 20/20 direction.

The establishment of mid-decade goals has been, in part, a manoeuvre to sustain the energy of the post-Summit process. In 1996, countries are due to report formally at the UN on their progress towards the goals for the year 2000. In many instances, this will be a report of some triumph: WHO reported on World Health Day in April 1995 that 146 countries have had no cases of polio for at least a year. Most of Asia has already made significant progress towards the goals, and many countries in East and South-East Asia have already achieved most of them.

Many countries in Latin America have also made considerable advances, as have many in the Middle East, albeit more selectively. In sub-Saharan Africa, the prospects are not good, though even there, with increased surveillance and national immunization campaigns, several countries will show improvement in at least half the goals.

But even with a renewed sense of commitment, it must be admitted that it will be difficult for many countries to bring about the reductions in child mortality, disease rates and illiteracy to which they committed themselves in 1990. Some African countries are in such a state of turmoil and economic crisis that for their leaders the vision of the Summit goals has already sunk below the horizon. UNICEF will, therefore, for the rest of the decade continue to put much of its energies into helping countries reach their child-centred targets.

The Convention on the Rights of the Child has already proved to be an effective framework for international action. With 179 countries having ratified it as of end-September 1995, universal ratification is within sight—and the focus is already shifting to implementation, encouraging all countries to live up to their most basic commitments to children. The Convention has evolved from a set of remote aspirational norms into a practical working instrument.

The Convention has established social and economic rights—the right to survival, early development, education, health care and social welfare support. It has also covered civil and political rights. These include the right of the child to a name and nationality, to freedom of expression, to participation in decisions affecting his or her well-being, and to protection from discrimination on grounds of gender, race or minority status, as well as protection from sexual and other forms of exploitation.

The key underlying advance is the recognition of the child as a complete individual. The Convention establishes that the child has an identity distinct from those of parents or nurturers and that the community has a duty to protect that identity and to enable the child to express it in matters such as guardianship or custody. In these areas, the overarching consideration should be "the best interests of the child."

In the early 1980s, the group of rights that UNICEF was most anxious to promote—and upon whose inclusion in the Convention it had insisted—were child rights to survival and development. The Convention asserts on behalf of children that their basic rights to health and education should ultimately be guaranteed by the State. When UNICEF could see those rights converging with the campaign for child survival and development, it gave the Convention energetic support both in the final drafting stages and

The Convention on the Rights of the Child recognizes the right of children to be protected against hazardous and exploitative labour, which is still the norm in many parts of the world.

UNICEF/93-0024/Murray-Lee

also after adoption by the General Assembly.

This happy twinning of the primary focus of UNICEF with the emergence of the Convention has given great power to the pursuit of children's issues in the 1990s. The goals remain at the heart of the agenda: they flow so organically from the Convention itself as to confer upon the Convention a special legitimacy. And because the goals operate within a specific time-frame, the Convention is blessed with an immediate applicability to the lives children lead.

UNICEF has actively pursued universal ratification, with the support of many NGOs. In the process, UNICEF has become strongly identified with the cause of child rights in ways that have important implications for its future work in both industrialized and developing countries. It has, for example, heightened its concern for children in especially difficult circumstances—abandoned children, children caught up in the violence of war, street children, children subject to special forms of abuse and discrimination and child victims of hazardous labour and sexual exploitation. To develop strategies to combat this most crushing form of exploitation, UNICEF is co-sponsoring the first ever World Congress on Commercial Sexual Exploitation of Children (Stockholm, August 1996).

This new attention to children's needs from a rights perspective means that in industrialized countries, as well as in the developing world, UNICEF has become much more of an advocate for children—injecting a new dimension into the work of its National Committees. UNICEF has also been supporting the work of the Committee on the Rights of the Child, the body that monitors ratifying countries as they move towards full implementation of the Convention.

The post-Summit process and the Convention on the Rights of the Child are helping to maintain the momentum on behalf of children. Even so, in the 1990s the prospects for the fight against poverty generally appear mixed. As in the case of progress towards the year 2000 goals, success in the struggle to ameliorate the human condition varies greatly between and among both regions and countries. While it is gratifying to recognize the substantial progress made in China, India and many other parts of Asia (which, after all, collectively represent half the world's children), it would be a mistake to fail to acknowledge that poverty is actually deepening in other regions of the world.

Early in the decade, the euphoria surrounding the immediate end of the cold war soon wore off. A world freed from the rigidities of superpower stand-off was now faced with the implosion of the USSR and the growing ethnic and nationalist turmoil in former Yugoslavia and elsewhere. In Europe, war re-emerged after an absence of 50 years, and those countries engaged in the transition from central planning to a free market found it a painful experience. The cold war thaw had briefly suggested that there might be a 'peace dividend' as expenditure on weapons was switched to development. But this idea vanished almost as soon as it had surfaced, and certainly did not long survive the costly hostilities of the Persian Gulf war.

In Africa, the 1990s have seen the end of apartheid in South Africa, with potential benefits for peace in the entire subregion, and a new development dynamism. However, the optimism this has generated has been counterbalanced by deepening crises elsewhere. Already during the 1980s, the continent had suffered from a seemingly endless

INDUSTRIALIZED COUNTRIES

▶ At the end of World War II, poor health and deprivation were common in many of today's industrialized countries. The infant mortality rate in southern Europe in the early 1950s was 80 per 1,000 births, twice as high as in Latin America today (38 per 1,000). Strong economic growth and the Welfare State reduced it dramatically.

▶ The number of children dying before age five declined from 43 to 9 per 1,000 between 1960 and 1993. Life expectancy rose from 67 to 77 years between 1950 and 1990.

▶ Primary education is universal; secondary enrolment reached 86 per cent in 1990.

▶ On average, a woman had 3.6 children in the early 1950s and 2 by 1975. In southern Europe, the sharpest decline came after 1975. In Spain, fertility has dropped from 2.9 to 1.2 over the last 20 years.

▶ Children in industrialized countries now face new problems, such as sharply increasing divorce rates, erosion of community, greater dependence on television and increasing alcohol and drug abuse.

▶ Slow economic growth, rising unemployment, worsening income distribution and more single-parent families have led to an increase in child poverty since 1980. In the US, an estimated 20 per cent of all children are defined as living in poverty.

UNICEF National Committees:
A network for children

UNICEF/5316/Horner

U NICEF is unique in the UN system in having a very sturdy, supportive network of private citizens— its National Committees. Currently, there are Committees for UNICEF in 38 industrialized countries. Autonomous non-governmental organizations (NGOs), they are recognized by their Governments and operate under formal relations with UNICEF. They vary in size, style and structure; some are nearly as old as UNICEF itself, and others have been formed within the last year. Yet all share a common purpose. They enable people, in their private capacities, to participate in United Nations efforts to save and improve the lives of children throughout the world.

The Committees are the main voice of UNICEF among the public in the richer countries. In addition to paid staff, they engage the efforts of more than 100,000 volunteers. They help raise awareness about the situation facing children in countries UNICEF assists and, increasingly, about the rights of children everywhere. In their own countries, they maintain contacts with the media, organize seminars, support education for development in schools and work with judicial, political and educational institutions on the development issues prioritized by UNICEF.

National Committees also raise funds. In 1994, they contributed almost 30 per cent of UNICEF's overall income. Indeed, of the top 15 donors to UNICEF, including governments, six are National Committees, some of which provided UNICEF with substantially larger contributions than their Governments.

The sole recipients of funds raised by the Committees have always been children in developing countries. The beneficiaries of Committees' knowledge and advocacy form a far broader group, however, including children in their own countries.

The Convention on the Rights of the Child enables Committees to work on rights issues that affect children in both industrialized and developing countries. Commercial sexual exploitation of children (including sex tourism), child labour, intercultural tolerance, the impact of war on children and the effects of land-mines on children are but a few of these.

A number of National Committees also were instrumental in the process leading to their governments' ratification of the Convention. Since then, many have become involved in the required formal process of governmental reporting on progress towards implementing the Convention.

Several Committees have helped form or have joined powerful coalitions of NGOs and other groups interested in child rights. These are becoming increasingly useful sources of knowledge and expertise for governments and interested citizens.

One example of the new role of Committees is their involvement in the movement against anti-personnel land-mines. In Belgium, Denmark, Ireland and Sweden, campaigns supported by Committees have prompted those Governments to move towards a total ban on anti-personnel mines. In Austria, France, Germany, Ireland and the United Kingdom, for example, public advocacy and political pressure by Committees and their NGO partners have forced Governments to propose much tougher restrictions on the use and supply of mines.

The National Committees have been crucial to UNICEF for decades. They help give form to a spontaneous human response to the plight of some of the world's most disadvantaged children.

Photo: The sole recipients of funds raised by National Committees are the children of the developing world.

succession of emergencies—mostly caused by, or associated with, drought. Africa's fortunes were further worsened by the continuing fall in commodity prices, which made it impossible for most countries to make much economic progress or shake off the heavy burden of debt. Worse was to follow in the form of political breakdown. In the 1990s, the collapse of frail political and administrative structures has pushed a number of countries—Liberia, Rwanda, Sierra Leone and Somalia—towards the ultimate condition of post-colonial breakdown: the 'failed State'.

In these emergency arenas, the children's agenda has been dominated by the combination of war with ongoing economic and environmental disaster. This has dashed developmental prospects and redirected attention towards specific child rights issues, in particular: children and land-mines, children and soldiering, and children lost or forced to flee because of fighting. In addition to considering what services children need, UNICEF has also been involved in the struggle to create humanitarian spaces—'zones of peace'—in which some minimum services at least can be delivered. To an organization born among the detritus of war, it sometimes seems as if the historical wheel has come full circle.

Towards 2000 and beyond

In a world whose post-colonial complexion has been radically transformed, the fight against world poverty can no longer be viewed uniformly. Global analyses of social and economic phenomena appear simplistic and often out of date. Increasingly refined methods of data collection, as well as careful situation analysis, programme planning and evaluation, all offer one clear message—that there is no such thing as a development formula.

Effective responses to problems of poverty have to derive from regional, national and local realities. The days of universal prescriptions are over. The keynotes for the future will be based on recognition of diversity—on adapting strategies to local circumstances and devolving decision-making so as to empower individuals and communities. This in turn will have a profound effect on future forms of international co-operation.

In many countries, the potential of health technology to improve the lives of children will largely have been realized before the end of the century. Polio has already been eliminated from the Americas and can be eliminated elsewhere. Guinea worm disease and iodine deficiency disorders are dwindling. The greater use of oral rehydration salts (ORS) means that diarrhoeal diseases such as cholera no longer represent the threat they once did; the greater availability of antibiotics means that respiratory infections are on the run. Other threats—malaria and AIDS— still remain, and the search for preventives and cures goes on.

But by the year 2000, it is conceivable that—in so far as it is technologically practicable—the promise of 'Health for All' will have been delivered. If that happens (though it remains a Herculean task), it will owe much to WHO and UNICEF, and the mobilizing power of the children's cause.

But other parts of the anti-poverty quest are more complex— and less susceptible to technical intervention. The eradication of such symptoms of poverty as illiteracy, environmental squalor, food insecurity and the exploitation of children in the workplace are challenges of a different order. That effort will benefit from the same kind of energy and commitment as

The keynotes for the future will be based on recognition of diversity— on adapting strategies to local circumstances and devolving decision-making so as to empower individuals and communities.

69

Fig. 12 Primary school enrolment rises

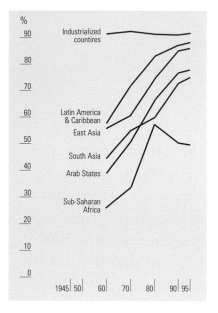

School enrolment of 6- to 11-year-olds improved greatly from 1950 to 1995 in all regions. Some gains were lost in the late 1980s and early 1990s in sub-Saharan Africa. However, the region's enrolment rate has still doubled over the last 45 years.

Fig. 13 Boys/girls enrolment gap narrows

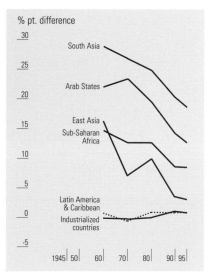

The gap between male and female primary school enrolment rates has narrowed between 1960 and 1995. In South Asia, the gap was nearly 30 points in 1960, dropping to 19 points in 1995. There and in the Arab States, however, the percentage point difference is still more than 10.

Source for both figures: UNESCO, *Trends and projections of enrolment by level of education, by age and by sex, 1960–2025* (as assessed in 1993), report BPE–94/WS.1, Paris, 1993.

was applied to the child health agenda. In that context, UNICEF has been systematically addressing each of those challenges, but they cannot just be mechanistically 'fixed'. They will demand significant changes in social attitudes and behaviours.

To some extent, the same is true even in the health area. All mass public health campaigns, however smart their technology, depend to a greater or lesser degree on the cooperative behaviour of human beings. And even the most effective health education and information campaigns tend to reach not more than a certain proportion of their target populations. That proportion may be very high: 80 per cent, 90 per cent, even 95 per cent for some vaccination campaigns.

In the case of some infectious agents, this may be enough to reduce their presence in a population to the point where the disease spontaneously dies out. In other cases, it will not.

The final 10 per cent of children or households still unreached by measles vaccine, or ORS packets, or sanitary latrines, or basic nutrition, may be as difficult to reach as the first 90 per cent—and also take as long and cost as much.

This final part of any campaign is usually a hard and grinding slog, with little of the glamour of the spectacular initial attack. 'Health for All' or 'Education for All' cannot be allowed to stop short at health or education for the majority. But it does demand a different approach—replacing the universalist philosophy with one that specifically identifies and targets the unreached.

This is where the twin movements on behalf of children—one based on 'rights', the other on 'needs'—coalesce.

The rights approach focuses on those who are disadvantaged by

denial of specific legally constituted rights. But reaching children with 'basic needs' will—under the terms of the Convention on the Rights of the Child—target a virtually identical group.

It is no coincidence that those children today categorized as being most vulnerable to society's depredations are the children in greatest need of, and with least access to, services of health, education and social welfare.

Those who are disadvantaged by unmet rights and those who are disadvantaged by unmet needs are ultimately the same children. Within the next few years, these two strands of disadvantage seem destined to mesh. And the implication is that, wherever the development quest goes, the world will still be looking in the direction of children and their future.

Over the past decade, children's emergence as a topic of public and political concern has been truly striking. In the past, the idea of statesmen sitting at a conference table to discuss the well-being of children would have been greeted with amazement if not derision. Compared with the waging of wars, the strength of the dollar, the price of oil, or the signing of NAFTAs or Maastrichts, the subject of children was regarded as trivial.

Indeed, times have changed. Most ministers and leaders around the world take the subject of children seriously. Today, the public policy agenda and the media in developing and industrialized countries alike are crowded with children's issues.

The 1990 World Summit for Children and the passage of the Convention on the Rights of the Child were symbols of that newfound prominence, and both have served to consolidate the presence of children and young people in political and social debate.

Girls' education: A lifeline to development

UNICEF/0071/Lemoyne

Education is one of the most critical areas of empowerment for women, as both the Cairo and Beijing conferences affirmed. It is also an area that offers some of the clearest examples of discrimination women suffer. Among children not attending school there are twice as many girls as boys, and among illiterate adults there are twice as many women as men.

Offering girls basic education is one sure way of giving them much greater power—of enabling them to make genuine choices over the kinds of lives they wish to lead. This is not a luxury. The Convention on the Rights of the Child and the Convention on the Elimination of All Forms of Discrimination against Women establish it as a basic human right.

That women might have the chance of a healthier and happier life should be reason enough for promoting girls' education. However, there are also important benefits for society as a whole. An educated woman has the skills, information and self-confidence that she needs to be a better parent, worker and citizen.

An educated woman is, for example, likely to marry at a later age and have fewer children. Cross-country studies show that an extra year of schooling for girls reduces fertility rates by 5 to 10 per cent. And the children of an educated mother are more likely to survive. In India, for example, the infant mortality rate of babies whose mothers have received primary education is half that of children whose mothers are illiterate.

An educated woman will also be more productive at work—and better paid. Indeed, the dividend for educational investment is often higher for women than men. Studies from a number of countries suggest that an extra year of schooling will increase a woman's future earnings by about 15 per cent, compared with 11 per cent for a man.

Over recent decades there has certainly been significant progress in girls' education. Between 1970 and 1992, combined primary and secondary enrolment for girls in developing countries rose from 38 per cent to 68 per cent—with particularly high rates in East Asia (83 per cent) and Latin America (87 per cent). But there is still some way to go. In the least developed countries enrolment rates are only 47 per cent at the primary level and 12 per cent at the secondary level.

What would it take to improve girls' access to education? Experience in scores of countries shows the importance, among other things, of:

▶ *Parental and community involvement*—Families and communities must be important partners with schools in developing curriculum and managing children's education.

▶ *Low-cost and flexible timetables*—Basic education should be free or cost very little. Where possible, there should be stipends and scholarships to compensate families for the loss of girls' household labour. Also, school hours should be flexible so children can help at home and still attend classes.

▶ *Schools close to home, with women teachers*—Many parents worry about girls travelling long distances on their own. Many parents also prefer to have daughters taught by women.

▶ *Preparation for school*—Girls do best when they receive early childhood care, which enhances their self-esteem and prepares them for school.

▶ *Relevant curricula*—Learning materials should be relevant to the girl's background and be in the local language. They should also avoid reproducing gender stereotypes.

Photo: A girl from the Miao indigenous group attends primary school in China.

71

Social goals: 1995 and 2000

Goals for 1995

The following goals were accepted by almost all nations for achievement by the end of 1995. Great progress has been made.

1 Immunization against the six major vaccine-preventable diseases of childhood to reach at least 80 per cent in all countries.

2 Neonatal tetanus to be virtually eliminated.

3 Measles deaths to be reduced by 95 per cent and measles cases by 90 per cent (compared with pre-immunization levels).

4 The elimination of polio in selected countries and regions (as a step towards worldwide elimination by the year 2000).

5 The ending of free or low-cost distribution of breastmilk substitutes in all maternity units and hospitals, and the achievement of 'baby-friendly' status for all major hospitals.

6 The achievement of 80 per cent ORT use, as part of the effort to control diarrhoeal disease.

7 The virtual elimination of vitamin A deficiency.

8 The universal iodization of salt in countries affected by iodine deficiency disorders.

9 The virtual elimination of guinea worm disease.

10 The universal ratification of the Convention on the Rights of the Child.

Goals for the year 2000

The end-of-century goals, agreed to by almost all the world's governments following the 1990 World Summit for Children, may be summarized under 10 priority points.

1 A one-third reduction in 1990 under-five death rates (or to 70 per 1,000 live births, whichever is less).

2 A halving of 1990 maternal mortality rates.

3 A halving of 1990 rates of malnutrition among the world's under-fives (to include the elimination of micronutrient deficiencies, support for breastfeeding by all maternity units, and a reduction in the incidence of low birth weight to less than 10 per cent).

4 The achievement of 90 per cent immunization among under-ones, the eradication of polio, the elimination of neonatal tetanus, a 90 per cent reduction in measles cases, and a 95 per cent reduction in measles deaths (compared with pre-immunization levels).

5 A halving of child deaths caused by diarrhoeal diseases.

6 A one-third reduction in child deaths from acute respiratory infections.

7 Basic education for all children and completion of primary education by at least 80 per cent—girls as well as boys.

8 Safe water and sanitation for all communities.

9 Acceptance by all countries of the Convention on the Rights of the Child, including improved protection for children in especially difficult circumstances.

10 Universal access to high-quality family planning information and services in order to prevent pregnancies that are too early, too closely spaced, too late or too many.

The attention today accorded to children is not just because they are society's 'most vulnerable citizens' or humanity's 'most precious resource'. Nor is it just because of their size as a demographic subgroup. This attention is being accorded to children in their own right. Partly this is a reflection of long-term changes in societies all over the world.

Decades of modernization and urbanization have changed many attitudes. As a result of this century's vast improvements in child survival and development, parents have greater hopes for their children, and they expect more for them. And society is investing much more in their education and training.

This is no accident. As we come to the end of the decade, the education of children, especially girls, has become one of the centre-pieces of international development. The principle that education brings empowerment, and with it the opportunity to transform life, has been affirmed, strongly, by the global conferences at Cairo, Copenhagen and Beijing. Seldom has the international community been so united as it is on the priority for universal primary education.

That is precisely what makes the future for children a realm of optimism rather than a crucible of despair. For the complex of reasons spanning 50 years, as set out in this report, it is now possible—in spite of the wars and the poverty—to believe that, ultimately, the world will not abandon, marginalize or depreciate children.

It has been a long struggle to have the lives of children taken seriously; it has consumed half a century to put children at the centre of the international development and human rights agenda.

But they are there, and nothing will now dislodge them. It is therefore possible to say, even amid the horrors of conflict and deprivation, that the 21st century will belong to children. It then remains to shape the policies and the programmes, the principles and the resources to give meaning to what has been achieved.

It is possible to say, even amid the horrors of conflict and deprivation, that the 21st century will belong to children.

UNICEF/93-0632/Press

The challenge of helping Africa protect its children remains, as many countries face natural emergencies such as drought, complicated by economic and political crises.

References

1   Cited in United Nations Children's Fund, *The State of the World's Children 1989*, UNICEF, New York, 1988, p. 87, and UNICEF, 1995.

2   United Nations Children's Fund and World Health Organization, 1994.

3   Sivard, Ruth Leger, *World Military and Social Expenditures 1993*, World Priorities Inc., Washington, D.C., 1993, p. 20.

4   UNICEF has compiled the estimates from a diversity of sources.

5   Ahlström, Christer, *Casualties of Conflict: Report for the world campaign for the protection of victims of war,* Department of Peace and Conflict Research, Uppsala, 1991, pp. 8, 19.

6   United Nations Research Institute for Social Development, *States of Disarray: The social effects of globalization,* UNRISD, 1995, p. 112.

7   This comment was broadcast over Radio Mille Collines in Rwanda. As many as 300,000 children were killed in the massacres in that country in 1994.

8   Ressler, Everett M., J. M. Tortorici and A. Marcelino, *Children in War: A guide to the provision of services,* UNICEF, New York, 1993, p. 117.

9   United Nations Research Institute for Social Development, *States of Disarray: The social effects of globalization,* op. cit., p. 113, box 7.1.

10   Stanley, Alessandra, 'Child Warriors', *Time,* 18 June 1990.

11   United Nations Children's Fund, *Hadlok: Filipino children caught in the crossfire,* UNICEF, Manila, undated, p. 15.

12   Dodge, Cole P., 'Child soldiers of Uganda and Mozambique', *Reaching Children in War: Sudan, Uganda and Mozambique,* edited by C. P. Dodge and M. Raundalen, Sigma Forlag, Uppsala, 1991, p. 54.

13   Macpherson, Martin, ed., *Child Soldiers: The recruitment of children into armed forces and their participation in hostilities,* Quaker Peace and Service Report, UK, updated September 1992, p. 11.

14   Ibid., p. 17.

15   United Nations Children's Fund, 'Angola: Alliance for life'. Document prepared for *The State of the World's Children 1996.* Luanda, July 1995, p. 4.

16   'Sierra Leone: Out of the bush', *The Economist,* 6 May 1995, pp. 41-42.

17   Macpherson, op. cit., p. 30.

18   Hammarberg, Thomas, presentation to the Regional Consultation on the Impact of Armed Conflict on Children in the Arab Region, in Cairo, 1995.

19   United Nations Children's Fund/United Nations Development Fund for Women, 'Women and Armed Conflict', in the kit on the Convention on the Elimination of All Forms of Discrimination against Women, UNICEF/UNIFEM, New York, 1995, p. 1.

20   El Bushra, Judy and E. Piza-Lopez, 'Gender, War and Food', in *War and Hunger: Rethinking international responses to complex emergencies,* edited by J. Macrae and A. Zwi, Zed Books, UK, 1994, p. 184.

21   Office of the United Nations High Commissioner for Refugees, *Refugees at a Glance: A monthly digest of UNHCR activities,* UNHCR, July 1995.

22   United Nations, *Update on the Nutrition Situation: A report compiled from information available to the ACC/SCN,* 1994, Geneva, November 1994, p. 58.

23   Ressler, op. cit., p. 142.

24   United Nations Children's Fund, 'Overview of Recent UNICEF Activities', Emergency Fund-raising Kit, update No. 4, October 1994.

25   United Nations Children's Fund, 'Angola: Alliance for life', op. cit., p. 3.

26   Zutt, Johannes, *Children of War: Wandering alone in southern Sudan,* UNICEF, New York, 1994, p. 1.

27   Boothby, Neil, 'Working in the War Zone: A look at psychological theory and practice from the field', *Mind and Human Interaction,* Vol. 2, No. 2, The Center for the Study of Mind and Human Interaction, October 1990, p. 34.

28   Ressler, op. cit., p. 145.

29   Ressler, op. cit., p. 97.

30   Green, Reginald Herbold, 'The Course of the Four Horsemen: The costs of war and its aftermath in sub-Saharan Africa: An overview', *War and Hunger,* edited by J. Macrae and A. Zwi, Zed Books, UK, 1994, p. 38.

31   Macrae, Joanna and A. Zwi, 'Famine, Complex Emergencies and International Policy in Africa: An overview', *War and Hunger,* edited by J. Macrae and A. Zwi, Zed Books, UK, 1994, p. 14.

32   Ibid., p. 19.

33   El Zein, Ali et al, *Situation Analysis and Surveys on Child Health in Lebanon,* UNICEF, Beirut, 1993, p. 18.

34   United Nations Children's Fund, 'Water, hygiene and sanitation', Emergency Operations in former Yugoslavia kit. UNICEF.

35   Dodge, Cole P., 'National and Societal Implications of War on Children', *Reaching Children in War: Sudan, Uganda and Mozambique,* op. cit., p. 11.

36   United Nations Children's Fund, *Children on the Front Line: The impact of apartheid, destabilization and warfare on children in southern and South Africa,* UNICEF, New York, 1989 update, p. 25.

37   *The New York Times,* 'UN Chief Chides Security Council on Military Missions', reported by Barbara Crossette, 6 January 1995.

38   United Nations Children's Fund, Iraq Emergency Country Profile, UNICEF, 1995.

39   United Nations Children's Fund, ' Psychosocial programme', Emergency Operations in former Yugoslavia kit, UNICEF; reference to data collected in Sarajevo in June and July 1993.

40   United Nations Children's Fund, 'Angola: Alliance for life', op. cit., pp. 3-4.

41   United Nations, The Sixth Periodic Report on the Situation of Human Rights in the Territory of former Yugoslavia, submitted by Tadeusz Mazowiecki, Special Rapporteur of the Commission on Human

Rights, E/CN.4/1994/110, UN Commission on Human Rights, Geneva, 21 February 1994, p. 34.

42 Ressler, op. cit., p. 174.

43 United Nations, The Sixth Periodic Report on the Situation of Human Rights in the Territory of former Yugoslavia, op. cit., p. 37.

44 United Nations Development Programme, *Human Development Report 1994*, UNDP, New York, 1994, p. 47, box 3.1.

45 Ibid., p. 59.

46 Sivard, op. cit., p. 42.

47 United Nations Development Programme, *Human Development Report 1994*, op. cit., pp. 50, 51.

48 Congressional Research Service, CRS Report for Congress, *Conventional Arms Transfers to Developing Nations, 1987-1994*, Washington, D.C., August 1995, p. 9.

49 Louise, Christopher, *The Social Impacts of Light Weapons Availability and Proliferation*, discussion paper prepared for UNRISD, International Alert, March 1995, p. 6.

50 United Nations, *Assistance in mine clearance: Report of the Secretary-General,* document A/49/357, United Nations, 6 September 1994, p. 7.

51 United Nations Children's Fund, *Anti-personnel land-mines: A scourge on children*, UNICEF, New York, 1994, p. 6.

52 Human Rights Watch/Africa, formerly Africa Watch, *Land-mines in Mozambique*, USA, March 1994.

53 Office of the United Nations High Commissioner for Refugees, statement by Sadako Ogata, High Commissioner, to the International Meeting on Mine Clearance, Geneva, 4 July 1995.

54 Guillermoprieto, Alma, 'The Shadow War', *The New York Review of Books*, 2 March 1995, p. 34.

55 Walker, Robert S., 'The Information Opportunity', *National Review*, 31 July 1995, p. 32.

56 Benthall, Jonathan, *Disasters, relief and the media*, I.B. Tauris, 1993, p. 102.

57 Hansen, Peter, 'Confronting Conflict', address delivered at a seminar, Wilton Park, Sussex, UK, 7 April 1995.

58 United Nations Development Programme, *Human Development Report 1994*, op. cit., p. 44.

59 Boutros-Ghali, Boutros, 'At 50, Does the UN Resemble the League of Nations?' *New Perspectives Quarterly*, Summer 1995, Vol. 12, No. 3, p. 37.

60 Vittachi, Varindra Tarzie, *Between the Guns: Children as a zone of peace*, Hodder and Stoughton, London, 1993, p. 9.

61 Black, Maggie, *Children First: The story of UNICEF past and present*, UNICEF/Oxford University Press, to be published in 1996.

62 United Nations Children's Fund, Report of the Executive Director, Overview of actions for children in 1987, E/ICEF/1988/2 (Part II), 23 February 1988, p. 4; and Report of the Executive Director, E/ICEF/1995/14 (Part II), 20 April 1995, p. 54.

63 United Nations Children's Fund, *Hadlok: Filipino children caught in the crossfire*, op. cit., p. 23.

64 United Nations, The Sixth Periodic Report on the Situation of Human Rights in the Territory of former Yugoslavia, op. cit., p. 36.

Glossary

AIDS
acquired immunodeficiency
syndrome

ASEAN
Association of South-East
Asian Nations

BCG
anti-tuberculosis vaccine

CEDC
children in especially difficult
circumstances

DDT
a chlorinated hydrocarbon
used as an insecticide

EPI
expanded programme on
immunization

FAO
Food and Agriculture Organization
of the United Nations

GDP
gross domestic product

GNP
gross national product

HIV
human immunodeficiency virus

ICRC
International Committee of the
Red Cross

IDD
iodine deficiency disorders

ILO
International Labour Organisation

IYC
International Year of the Child

LAS
League of Arab States

NAFTA
North American Free Trade
Agreement

NGO
non-governmental organization

NPA
national programme of action

OAS
Organization of American States

OAU
Organization of African Unity

OIC
Organization of the Islamic
Conference

OLS
Operation Lifeline Sudan

OPEC
Organization of Petroleum
Exporting Countries

ORS
oral rehydration salts

ORT
oral rehydration therapy

PHC
primary health care

SAARC
South Asian Association for
Regional Cooperation

UCI
universal child immunization

U5MR
under-five mortality rate

UN
United Nations

UNDP
United Nations Development
Programme

UNESCO
United Nations Educational,
Scientific and Cultural Organization

UNFPA
United Nations Population Fund

UNHCR
Office of the United Nations High
Commissioner for Refugees

UNICEF
United Nations Children's Fund

UNRRA
United Nations Relief and
Rehabilitation Administration

WHO
World Health Organization

Statistical tables

Economic and social statistics on the nations of the world, with particular reference to children's well-being.

General note on the data

The data provided in these tables are accompanied by definitions, sources and explanations of symbols. Tables derived from so many sources—12 major sources are listed in the explanatory material—will inevitably cover a wide range of data quality. Official government data received by the responsible United Nations agency have been used whenever possible. In the many cases where there are no reliable official figures, estimates made by the responsible United Nations agency have been used. Where such internationally standardized estimates do not exist, the tables draw on other sources, particularly data received from the appropriate UNICEF field office. Where possible, only comprehensive or representative national data have been used.

Data quality is likely to be adversely affected for countries that have recently suffered from man-made or natural disasters. This is particularly so where basic country infrastructure has been fragmented or major population movements have occurred.

Data for life expectancy, crude birth and death rates, infant mortality rates, etc. are part of the regular work on estimates and projections undertaken by the United Nations Population Division. These and other internationally produced estimates are revised periodically, which explains why some of the data will differ from those found in earlier UNICEF publications.

Data for ORT use are undergoing review at WHO and UNICEF, so—with few exceptions—data appearing in table 3 of *The State of the World's Children 1995* have been repeated this year.

Explanation of symbols

Since the aim of this statistics chapter is to provide a broad picture of the situation of children and women worldwide, detailed data qualifications and footnotes are seen as more appropriate for inclusion elsewhere. Only two symbols are used in the tables.

.. Data not available.

x Indicates data that refer to years or periods other than those specified in the column heading, differ from the standard definition, or refer to only part of a country.

Note: Child mortality estimates for individual countries are primarily derived from data reported by the United Nations Population Division. In some cases, these estimates may differ from the latest national figures. In general, data released during approximately the last year are not incorporated in these estimates.

Index to countries

In the following tables, countries are ranked in descending order of their estimated 1994 under-five mortality rate. The reference numbers indicating that rank are given in the alphabetical list of countries below.

Table 1: Basic indicators

		Under-5 mortality rate		Infant mortality rate (under 1)		Total population (millions)	Annual no. of births (thousands)	Annual no. of under-5 deaths (thousands)	GNP per capita (US$)	Life expectancy at birth (years)	Total adult literacy rate	Primary school enrolment ratio (gross)	% share of household income 1980-93	
		1960	1994	1960	1994	1994	1994	1994	1993	1994	1990	1986-93	lowest 40%	highest 20%
1	Niger	320	**320**	191	191	8.9	459	147	270	46	12	29	..	..
2	Angola	345	**292**	208	170	10.7	542	158	700	46	42	91	..	..
3	Sierra Leone	385	**284**	219	164	4.4	214	61	150	39	27	48	..	..
4	Mozambique	331	**277**	190	161	15.5	699	194	90	46	35	60	..	..
5	Afghanistan	360	**257**	215	165	18.9	970	249	280x	43	27	24	..	..
6	Guinea-Bissau	336	**231**	200	137	1.1	44	10	240	43	50	60	9	59
7	Guinea	337	**223**	203	131	6.5	326	73	500	44	31	42	..	..
8	Malawi	365	**221**	206	140	10.8	535	118	200	46	52x	66	..	..
9	Liberia	288	**217**	192	144	2.9	138	30	450x	55	34	35	..	..
10	Mali	400	**214**	233	119	10.5	525	112	270	46	25	25	..	..
11	Gambia	375	**213**	213	129	1.1	46	10	350	45	34	69	..	..
12	Somalia	294	**211**	175	125	9.1	458	97	120x	47	24	11x	..	..
13	Zambia	220	**203**	135	114	9.2	402	82	380	49	73	95	15	50
14	Chad	325	**202**	195	119	6.2	269	54	210	47	43	65	..	..
15	Eritrea	294	**200**	175	117	3.4	146	29	100	50	..	..	..	..
16	Ethiopia	294	**200**	175	117	53.4	2562	511	100	47	31x	22	21	41
17	Mauritania	321	**199**	191	114	2.2	87	17	500	51	35	62	14	46
18	Bhutan	324	**193**	203	125	1.6	64	12	170	50	37	25	..	..
19	Nigeria	204	**191**	122	114	108.5	4855	927	300	50	49	76	15	49
20	Zaire	286	**186**	167	120	42.6	2002	372	220x	52	72	70	..	..
21	Uganda	218	**185**	129	111	20.6	1055	195	180	45	57	80	21	42
22	Cambodia	217	**177**	146	113	10.0	417	74	200x	51	35	..	..	..
23	Burundi	255	**176**	151	106	6.2	281	50	180	50	31	69	..	..
24	Central African Rep.	294	**175**	174	103	3.2	133	23	400	49	50	68	..	..
25	Burkina Faso	318	**169**	183	89	10.1	465	79	300	47	16	37	..	..
26	Madagascar	364	**164**	219	100	14.3	616	101	220	56	80	79	..	..
27	Tanzania, U. Rep. of	249	**159**	147	105	28.9	1228	195	90	52	62x	68	8	63
28	Lesotho	204	**156**	138	106	2.0	73	11	650	60	67	106	9	60
29	Gabon	287	**151**	171	91	1.3	49	7	4960	53	56	..	..	..
30	Côte d'Ivoire	300	**150**	195	90	13.8	682	102	630	51	34	69	18	44
31	Benin	310	**142**	184	85	5.3	253	36	430	47	30	66	..	..
32	Rwanda	191	**139**	115	80	7.8	340	47	210	47	54	77	23	39
33	Lao Peo. Dem. Rep.	233	**138**	155	94	4.7	211	29	280	51	52x	98	..	..
34	Pakistan	221	**137**	137	95	136.7	5461	748	430	61	34	46	21	40
35	Togo	264	**132**	155	83	4.0	177	23	340	55	45	111	..	..
36	Ghana	213	**131**	126	76	16.9	695	91	430	56	58	74	18	44
37	Haiti	260	**127**	170	74	7.0	246	31	370x	56	41	56	..	..
38	Sudan	292	**122**	170	74	27.4	1078	131	480x	53	40	51	..	..
39	India	236	**119**	144	79	918.6	26095	3103	300	60	48	102	21	41
40	Nepal	290	**118**	190	84	21.4	827	98	190	53	24	102	22	40
41	Bangladesh	247	**117**	151	91	117.8	4127	483	220	55	35	77	23	39
42	Senegal	303	**115**	174	60	8.1	344	40	750	49	29	59	11	59
43	Yemen	340	**112**	230	78	13.9	670	75	520x	50	39	78	..	..
44	Indonesia	216	**111**	127	71	194.6	4684	520	740	62	82	115	21	42
45	Bolivia	252	**110**	152	73	7.2	255	28	760	59	79	85	15	48
46	Cameroon	264	**109**	156	69	12.9	520	57	820	56	57	101	..	..
47	Congo	220	**109**	143	82	2.5	112	12	950	51	68	..	..	..
48	Myanmar	237	**109**	158	79	45.6	1457	159	220x	57	81	105	..	..
49	Libyan Arab Jamahiriya	269	**95**	160	64	5.2	216	21	5310x	63	70	..	..	..
50	Papua New Guinea	248	**95**	165	67	4.2	139	13	1130	56	68	73	..	..
51	Kenya	202	**90**	120	61	27.3	1201	108	270	56	72	95	10	62
52	Turkmenistan	..	**87**	..	70	4.0	124	11	1230x	65	98x	..	..	..
53	Tajikistan	..	**81**	..	63	5.9	212	17	470	70	98x	..	..	..
54	Zimbabwe	181	**81**	109	57	11.0	421	34	520	54	82	119	10	62
55	Namibia	206	**78**	129	62	1.5	55	4	1820	59	..	124	..	..
56	Mongolia	185	**76**	128	58	2.4	63	5	390	63	80	89	..	..
57	Iraq	171	**71**	117	57	19.9	751	54	1036x	66	52	89	..	..
58	Guatemala	205	**70**	137	51	10.3	393	28	1100	65	53	79	8	63
59	South Africa	126	**68**	89	52	40.6	1247	85	2980	63	80x	109	9	63
60	Nicaragua	209	**68**	140	49	4.3	168	11	340	66	64x	102	12	55
61	Algeria	243	**65**	148	54	27.3	775	50	1780	67	55	99	18	47
62	Uzbekistan	..	**64**	..	52	22.4	678	43	970	69	97x	..	..	..
63	Brazil	181	**61**	118	51	159.1	3824	233	2930	66	81	106	7	68
64	Peru	236	**58**	143	41	23.3	627	36	1490	66	86	119	14	51
65	Philippines	102	**57**	73	44	66.2	1968	112	850	66	94	109	17	48
66	Ecuador	180	**57**	115	45	11.2	308	17	1200	69	87	116	..	..
67	El Salvador	210	**56**	130	42	5.6	187	11	1320	66	69	78	..	..
68	Morocco	215	**56**	133	46	26.5	746	42	1040	63	39	69	17	46
69	Kyrgyzstan	..	**56**	..	47	4.7	130	7	850	69	96x	..	10	57
70	Turkey	217	**55**	161	47	60.8	1608	88	2970	66	79	113	..	..
71	Botswana	170	**54**	117	42	1.4	53	3	2790	65	66	116	11	59
72	Honduras	203	**54**	137	41	5.5	199	11	600	67	69	105	9	64
73	Egypt	258	**52**	169	41	61.6	1733	90	660	63	48	101	..	..
74	Azerbaijan	..	**51**	..	35	7.5	159	8	730	70	97x	..	..	..
75	Iran, Islamic Rep. of	233	**51**	145	40	65.8	2244	114	2200x	67	62	109	..	..

		Under-5 mortality rate		Infant mortality rate (under 1)		Total population (millions) 1994	Annual no. of births (thousands) 1994	Annual no. of under-5 deaths (thousands) 1994	GNP per capita (US$) 1993	Life expectancy at birth (years) 1994	Total adult literacy rate 1990	Primary school enrolment ratio (gross) 1986-93	% share of household income 1980-93	
		1960	1994	1960	1994								lowest 40%	highest 20%
76	Kazakhstan	..	**48**	..	41	17.0	323	16	1560	70	97x	..	..	..
77	Viet Nam	219	**46**	147	35	72.9	2194	101	170	65	91	108	19	44
78	Dominican Rep.	152	**45**	104	38	7.7	200	9	1230	69	80	95	12	56
79	China	209	**43**	140	35	1208.8	21513	925	490	68	78	121	17	42
80	Albania	151	**41**	112	34	3.4	79	3	340	72	..	101	..	..
81	Lebanon	85	**40**	65	33	2.9	76	3	2150x	68	91	111	..	..
82	Syrian Arab Rep.	201	**38**	136	32	14.2	574	22	1160x	67	66	107	..	..
83	Moldova	..	**36**	..	31	4.4	67	2	1060	68	96x	..	..	..
84	Saudi Arabia	292	**36**	170	31	17.5	618	22	7510x	69	59	78	..	..
85	Paraguay	90	**34**	66	28	4.8	155	5	1510	70	91	110	..	..
86	Tunisia	244	**34**	163	28	8.7	215	7	1720	68	60	120	16	46
87	Thailand	146	**32**	101	27	58.2	1102	36	2110	69	93	97	15	51
88	Armenia		**32**		27	3.6	70	2	660	72	99x	..	..	..
89	TFYR Macedonia	177	**32**	120	27	2.1	32	1	820	72	..	..	..	..
90	Mexico	148	**32**	103	27	91.9	2473	79	3610	71	88	113	12	56
91	Russian Federation	..	**31**	..	28	147.4	1487	46	2340	68	99x	..	14	48
92	Korea, Dem. Peo. Rep.	120	**31**	85	23	23.5	559	17	970x	71	..	104	..	..
93	Romania	82	**29**	69	23	22.9	245	7	1140	70	97x	88	..	..
94	Georgia	..	**27**	..	23	5.5	84	2	580	73	99x	..	..	..
95	Argentina	68	**27**	57	24	34.2	685	18	7220	72	96	107	..	..
96	Oman	300	**27**	180	22	2.1	90	2	4850	69	..	100	..	..
97	Latvia	..	**26**	..	22	2.6	28	1	2010	69	99x	86	..	..
98	Ukraine	..	**25**	..	21	51.5	568	14	2210	70	98x	..	..	..
99	Jordan	149	**25**	103	21	5.2	199	5	1190	68	82	105	17	48
100	Venezuela	70	**24**	53	20	21.4	568	13	2840	72	90	99	14	50
101	Estonia	..	**23**	..	20	1.5	16	0	3080	69	100x	85	..	..
102	Yugoslavia	120	**23**	87	20	10.8	149	3	a	72	..	..	..	..
103	Mauritius	84	**23**	62	19	1.1	23	1	3030	70	80	106	..	..
104	Belarus	..	**21**	..	18	10.2	116	2	2870	70	98x	..	..	..
105	Uruguay	47	**21**	41	19	3.2	54	1	3830	72	97	108	..	..
106	United Arab Emirates	240	**20**	160	17	1.9	41	1	21430	74	77x	118	..	..
107	Lithuania	..	**20**	..	17	3.7	48	1	1320	71	98x	92	..	..
108	Panama	104	**20**	67	18	2.6	63	1	2600	73	89	105	8	60
109	Trinidad and Tobago	73	**20**	61	17	1.3	26	1	3830	71	97x	95	..	..
110	Bulgaria	70	**19**	49	16	8.8	89	2	1140	71	..	90	21	39
111	Sri Lanka	130	**19**	90	15	18.1	367	7	600	72	89	107	22	39
112	Colombia	132	**19**	82	16	34.6	808	15	1400	69	90	117	11	56
113	Bosnia and Herzegovina	155	**17**	105	15	3.5	48	1	b	72	..	..	..	..
114	Poland	70	**16**	62	14	38.3	494	8	2260	71	99x	98	23	36
115	Costa Rica	112	**16**	80	14	3.4	86	1	2150	76	94	105	13	51
116	Chile	138	**15**	107	13	14.0	300	5	3170	74	94	96	10	60
117	Slovakia	..	**15**	..	13	5.3	75	1	1950	71	..	..	..	..
118	Malaysia	105	**15**	73	12	19.7	545	8	3140	71	80	93	13	54
119	Croatia	98	**14**	70	12	4.5	50	1	a	71	..	..	..	..
120	Hungary	57	**14**	51	13	10.2	120	2	3350	69	99x	89	26	34
121	Kuwait	128	**14**	89	12	1.6	42	1	19360	75	76	60	16	48
122	Jamaica	76	**13**	58	10	2.4	51	1	1440	73	83	106	16	48
123	Portugal	112	**11**	81	9	9.8	118	1	9130	75	85	120	..	..
124	Cuba	50	**10**	39	9	11.0	180	2	1170x	75	94	102	..	..
125	United States	30	**10**	26	8	260.6	4080	41	24740	76	..	104	16	42
126	Czech Rep.	..	**10**	..	9	10.3	136	1	2710	71	..	..	..	..
127	Belgium	35	**10**	31	8	10.1	121	1	21650	76	..	99	22x	36x
128	Greece	64	**10**	53	8	10.4	102	1	7390	78	93	97	..	..
129	Spain	57	**9**	46	8	39.6	378	4	13590	78	95	107	22	37
130	France	34	**9**	29	7	57.8	736	7	22490	77	..	106	17	42
131	Israel	39	**9**	32	7	5.5	111	1	13920	76	92x	94	18x	40x
132	New Zealand	26	**9**	22	7	3.5	60	1	12600	75	..	104	16	45
133	Korea, Rep. of	124	**9**	88	8	44.6	732	6	7660	71	97	102	20	42
134	Slovenia	45	**8**	37	7	1.9	20	0	6490	73	..	..	..	..
135	Australia	24	**8**	20	7	17.9	262	2	17500	77	..	107	16	42
136	Italy	50	**8**	44	7	57.2	557	4	19840	77	97	95	19	41
137	Netherlands	22	**8**	18	6	15.4	199	2	20950	77	..	98	21	37
138	Norway	23	**8**	19	6	4.3	62	0	25970	77	..	99	19x	37x
139	Canada	33	**8**	28	6	29.1	435	3	19970	77	97x	107	18	40
140	Austria	43	**7**	37	6	7.9	94	1	23510	76	..	104	..	..
141	United Kingdom	27	**7**	23	6	58.1	777	6	18060	76	..	104	15	44
142	Switzerland	27	**7**	22	6	7.1	90	1	35760	78	..	105	17	45
143	Ireland	36	**7**	31	6	3.5	52	0	13000	75	..	103	..	..
144	Germany	40	**7**	34	6	81.3	778	5	23560	76	..	94	19	40
145	Denmark	25	**7**	22	6	5.2	65	0	26730	75	..	95	17	39
146	Japan	40	**6**	31	4	124.8	1259	8	31490	79	..	102	22x	38x
147	Hong Kong	52	**6**	38	5	5.8	63	0	18060	79	91x	104x	16	47
148	Singapore	40	**6**	31	5	2.8	43	0	19850	75	89x	107	15	49
149	Finland	28	**5**	22	4	5.1	66	0	19300	76	..	100	18	38
150	Sweden	20	**5**	16	4	8.7	124	1	24740	78	..	101	21	37

Countries listed in descending order of their under-five mortality rates (shown in bold type).
a: Range US$696 to US$2785.   b: Range US$695 or less.

Table 2: Nutrition

		% of infants with low birth weight 1990	% of children (1986-94) who are: exclusively breastfed (0-3 months)	breastfed with complementary food (6-9 months)	still breastfeeding (20-23 months)	% of under-fives (1980-94) suffering from: underweight moderate & severe	severe	wasting moderate & severe	stunting moderate & severe	Total goitre rate (6-11 years) (%) 1980-92	Daily per capita calorie supply as a % of requirements 1988-90	% share of total household consumption (1980-85) all food	cereals
1	Niger	15	..	..	..	36	12	16	32	9	95	..	..
2	Angola	19	3	83	53	..	..	..	..	7	80	..	..
3	Sierra Leone	17	..	94	41	29	..	9x	35	7	83	56	22
4	Mozambique	20	..	..	..	..	..	..	..	20	77	..	..
5	Afghanistan	20	..	..	..	..	..	..	..	20	72	..	..
6	Guinea-Bissau	20	..	..	..	23x	..	..	..	19	97	..	..
7	Guinea	21	..	..	..	..	..	..	..	19	97	..	..
8	Malawi	20	3	88	56	27	8	5	49	13	88	30	9
9	Liberia	..	15	56	26	20x	..	3x	37x	6	98	..	..
10	Mali	17	8	45	44	31x	9x	11x	24x	29	96	57	22
11	Gambia	..	..	..	61	..	..	..	..	..	..	..	..
12	Somalia	16	..	..	..	..	..	..	..	7	81	..	..
13	Zambia	13	13	88	34	25	6	5	40	51x	87	36	8
14	Chad	..	..	..	..	..	..	..	..	15	73	..	..
15	Eritrea	..	..	..	..	..	..	..	..	..	..	..	..
16	Ethiopia	16	74	..	35	48x	16x	8x	64x	22	73	49	24
17	Mauritania	11	12	39	..	48	..	16	57	..	106	..	..
18	Bhutan	..	..	..	..	38	..	4	56	25	128	..	..
19	Nigeria	16	2	52	43	36	12	9	43	10	93	48	18
20	Zaire	15	..	..	..	28x	..	5x	43x	9	96	..	..
21	Uganda	..	63	71	24	23	5	2	45	7	93	..	..
22	Cambodia	..	..	..	..	40	7	8	38	15	96	..	..
23	Burundi	..	89	66	73	38x	10x	6x	48x	42	84	..	..
24	Central African Rep.	15	..	..	..	..	..	..	..	63	82	..	..
25	Burkina Faso	21x	3	44	..	30	8	13	29	16	94	..	..
26	Madagascar	17	47	80	45	39	9	5	51	24	95	59	26
27	Tanzania, U. Rep. of	14	32	59	57	29	7	6	47	37	95	64	32
28	Lesotho	11	..	..	..	16	2	5	26	16	93	..	..
29	Gabon	..	..	..	..	..	..	..	..	5	104	..	..
30	Côte d'Ivoire	14x	..	..	..	12	2	9	17	6	111	39	13
31	Benin	..	..	..	..	..	..	..	..	24	104	37	12
32	Rwanda	17	90	68	..	29	6	4	48	49	82	29	10
33	Lao Peo. Dem. Rep.	18	..	..	..	37	..	11	40	25	111	..	..
34	Pakistan	25	25	29	52	40	14	9	50	32	99	37	12
35	Togo	20	10	86	68	24x	6x	5x	30x	22	99	..	..
36	Ghana	17	8	36	53	27	8	11	26	10	93	50	..
37	Haiti	15	3	..	..	27	3x	5	34	4	89	..	..
38	Sudan	15	14	45	44	20	..	14	32	20	87	60	..
39	India	33	51	31	67	69x	27x	..	65x	9	101	52	18
40	Nepal	..	..	..	..	70x	5x	14x	69x	44	100	57	38
41	Bangladesh	50	54	..	..	67	25	17	63	11	88	59	36
42	Senegal	11	7	41	48	20	5	9	22	12	98	49	15
43	Yemen	19	15	51	..	30	4	13	44	32	..	..	..
44	Indonesia	14	47	76	62	40	..	..	..	28	121	48	21
45	Bolivia	12	53	78	36	16	4	4	28	21	84	33	..
46	Cameroon	13	7	77	35	14	3	3	24	26	95	24	7
47	Congo	16	43	..	27	24	..	5	27	8	103	37	16
48	Myanmar	16	..	..	..	32x	9x	..	..	18	114	..	..
49	Libyan Arab Jamahiriya	..	..	..	..	..	..	..	..	6	140	..	..
50	Papua New Guinea	23	..	..	..	35	..	..	..	30	114	..	..
51	Kenya	16	17	90	54	22	6	6	33	7	89	38	16
52	Turkmenistan	..	..	..	..	..	..	..	..	20	..	..	..
53	Tajikistan	..	..	..	..	..	..	..	..	20	..	..	..
54	Zimbabwe	14	11	94	26	12x	2x	1x	29x	42	94	40	9
55	Namibia	16	22	65	23	26	6	9	28	35	..	..	..
56	Mongolia	10	..	..	..	12x	..	2x	26x	7	97	..	..
57	Iraq	15	..	..	..	12	2	3	22	7	128	..	..
58	Guatemala	14	..	..	44	34x	8x	1x	58x	20	103	36	10
59	South Africa	..	..	..	..	..	..	..	25	2	128	34	..
60	Nicaragua	15	..	..	..	12	1	2	24	4	99	..	..
61	Algeria	9	..	..	..	9	..	6	18	9	123	..	..
62	Uzbekistan	..	..	..	..	..	..	..	..	18	..	..	..
63	Brazil	11	4	27	13	7	1	2	16	14x	114	35	9
64	Peru	11	40	62	36	11	2	1	37	36	87	35	8
65	Philippines	15	33	52	18	34	5	6	37	15	104	51	21
66	Ecuador	11	31	31	23	17	0	2	34	10	105	30	..
67	El Salvador	11	20	71	28	11	1	1	23	25	102	33	12
68	Morocco	9	65	35	..	9	2	2	23	20	125	38	12
69	Kyrgyzstan	..	..	..	..	..	..	..	..	20	..	..	..
70	Turkey	8	..	..	..	10	2	3	21	36	127	40	9
71	Botswana	8	41	82	23	15x	..	..	44	8	97	25	12
72	Honduras	9	11	..	..	21	4	2	39	9	98	39	..
73	Egypt	10	38	52	..	9	2	3	24	5	132	49	10
74	Azerbaijan	..	..	..	..	..	..	..	..	20	..	..	..
75	Iran, Islamic Rep. of	9	..	..	..	..	..	..	..	30	125	37	10

		% of infants with low birth weight 1990	% of children (1986-94) who are: exclusively breastfed (0-3 months)	breastfed with complementary food (6-9 months)	still breastfeeding (20-23 months)	% of under-fives (1980-94) suffering from: underweight moderate & severe	underweight severe	wasting moderate & severe	stunting moderate & severe	Total goitre rate (6-11 years) (%) 1980-92	Daily per capita calorie supply as a % of requirements 1988-90	% share of total household consumption (1980-85) all food	cereals
76	Kazakhstan	..	..	..	..	..	..	..	..	20	..	..	..
77	Viet Nam	17	..	..	..	42	14	6	51	20	103	..	..
78	Dominican Rep.	16	10	32	7	10	2	1	19	..	102	46	13
79	China	9	..	..	..	17	3x	4x	32x	..	112	61	..
80	Albania	7	..	..	..	..	..	..	..	41	107	..	..
81	Lebanon	10	..	..	..	..	..	..	..	15	127	..	..
82	Syrian Arab Rep.	11	..	..	..	..	..	..	..	73	126	..	..
83	Moldova	..	..	..	..	..	..	..	..	..	..	..	..
84	Saudi Arabia	7	..	..	..	..	..	..	..	..	121	..	..
85	Paraguay	8	7	61	8	4	1	0	17	49	116	30	6
86	Tunisia	8	12	53	16	10x	2x	3x	18x	4	131	37	7
87	Thailand	13	4	69	34	26x	4x	6x	22x	12	103	30	7
88	Armenia	..	..	..	..	..	..	..	..	10	..	..	..
89	TFYR Macedonia	..	..	..	..	..	..	..	..	..	..	..	..
90	Mexico	12	37	36	21	14	..	6	22	15	131	35	..
91	Russian Federation	..	..	..	..	..	..	..	..	..	..	..	..
92	Korea, Dem. Peo. Rep.	..	..	..	..	..	..	..	..	..	121	..	..
93	Romania	7	..	..	..	..	..	..	..	10	116	..	..
94	Georgia	..	..	..	..	..	..	..	..	20	..	..	..
95	Argentina	6	..	..	..	..	..	..	..	8	131	35	4
96	Oman	10	..	..	..	..	..	..	..	..	..	..	..
97	Latvia	..	..	..	..	..	..	..	..	..	..	..	..
98	Ukraine	..	..	..	..	..	..	..	..	10	..	..	..
99	Jordan	7	32	48	13	9	..	2	16	..	110	35	..
100	Venezuela	9	..	..	..	6	..	2	6	11	99	23	..
101	Estonia	..	..	..	..	..	..	..	..	..	..	..	..
102	Yugoslavia	..	..	..	..	..	..	..	..	..	..	..	..
103	Mauritius	9	16	29	..	24	..	16	22	..	128	24	7
104	Belarus	..	..	..	..	..	..	..	..	22	..	..	..
105	Uruguay	8	..	..	..	7	2	..	16	..	101	31	7
106	United Arab Emirates	6	..	..	26	..	..	..	..	..	..	..	..
107	Lithuania	..	..	..	..	..	..	..	..	..	..	..	..
108	Panama	10	..	..	..	7	1	1	9	.13	98	38	7
109	Trinidad and Tobago	10	10	39	16	7x	0x	4x	5x	..	114	19	3
110	Bulgaria	6	..	..	..	..	..	..	..	20	148	..	..
111	Sri Lanka	25	14	47	46	38	3x	16	24	14	101	43	18
112	Colombia	10	17	48	24	10	2	3	17	10	106	29	..
113	Bosnia and Herzegovina	..	..	..	..	..	..	..	..	..	..	..	..
114	Poland	..	..	..	..	..	..	..	..	10	131	29	4
115	Costa Rica	6	..	..	..	2	0	2	8	3	121	33	8
116	Chile	7	..	..	..	3x	..	1x	10x	9	102	29	7
117	Slovakia	..	..	..	..	..	..	..	..	..	..	..	..
118	Malaysia	10	..	..	..	23	1	..	..	20	120	23	..
119	Crotia	..	..	..	..	..	..	..	..	..	..	..	..
120	Hungary	9	..	..	..	..	..	..	..	..	137	25	3
121	Kuwait	7	..	..	..	6	..	3	12	..	114	36	14
122	Jamaica	11	..	..	..	9	1	1	5	..	..	..	..
123	Portugal	5	..	..	..	..	..	..	..	15	136	34	8
124	Cuba	9	..	..	..	..	..	1	..	10	135	..	..
125	United States	7	..	..	..	..	..	..	..	..	138	10	2
126	Czech Rep.	..	..	..	..	..	..	..	..	..	..	..	..
127	Belgium	6	..	..	..	..	..	..	..	5	149	15	2
128	Greece	6	..	..	..	..	..	..	..	10	151	30	3
129	Spain	4	..	..	..	..	..	..	..	10	141	24	3
130	France	5	..	..	..	..	..	..	..	5	143	16	2
131	Israel	7	..	..	..	..	..	..	..	..	125	21	..
132	New Zealand	6	..	..	..	..	..	..	..	..	131	12	2
133	Korea, Rep. of	9	..	..	..	..	..	..	..	..	120	35	14
134	Slovenia	..	..	..	..	..	..	..	..	..	..	..	..
135	Australia	6	..	..	..	..	..	..	..	..	124	13	..
136	Italy	5	..	..	..	..	..	..	..	20	139	19	2
137	Netherlands	..	..	..	..	..	..	..	..	3	114	13	2
138	Norway	4	..	..	..	..	..	..	..	..	120	15	2
139	Canada	6	..	..	..	..	..	..	..	..	122	11	2
140	Austria	6	..	..	..	..	..	..	..	..	133	16	2
141	United Kingdom	7	..	..	..	..	..	..	..	..	130	12	2
142	Switzerland	5	..	..	..	..	..	..	..	..	130	17	..
143	Ireland	4	..	..	..	..	..	..	..	..	157	22	4
144	Germany	..	..	..	..	..	..	..	..	10	..	12	2
145	Denmark	6	..	..	..	..	..	..	..	5	135	13	2
146	Japan	6	..	..	..	..	..	..	..	..	125	17	4
147	Hong Kong	8	..	..	..	..	..	..	..	..	125	12	1
148	Singapore	7	..	..	..	14x	..	4x	11x	..	136	19	..
149	Finland	4	..	..	..	..	..	..	..	..	113	16	3
150	Sweden	5	..	..	..	..	..	..	..	..	111	13	2

Countries listed in descending order of their 1994 under-five mortality rates (table 1).

Table 3: Health

		% of population with access to safe water 1990-95			% of population with access to adequate sanitation 1990-95			% of population with access to health services 1985-95			% fully immunized 1990-94 1-year-old children				pregnant women tetanus	ORT use rate 1990-94
		total	urban	rural	total	urban	rural	total	urban	rural	TB	DPT	polio	measles		
1	Niger	54	46	55	15	71	4	32	99	30	32	20	20	19	44	17
2	Angola	32	69	15	16	34	8	30x	..	..	48	27	28	44	18	48
3	Sierra Leone	34	58	21	11	17	8	38	90	20	60	43	43	46	61	60
4	Mozambique	33	17	40	20x	61x	11x	39	100	30	78	55	55	65	37	60
5	Afghanistan	12	39	5	..	13	..	29	80	17	44	18	18	40	6	26
6	Guinea-Bissau	53	38	57	21	32	17	40	..	..	95	74	68	65	55	26
7	Guinea	55	50	56	21	84	10	80	100	70	75	70	70	70	56	82
8	Malawi	47x	91x	42x	53	71	51	80	..	..	99	98	98	98	76	50
9	Liberia	46	79	13	30	56	4	39	50	30	84	43	45	44	35	15
10	Mali	37	36	38	31	58	21	30	..	..	67	39	39	46	6	10
11	Gambia	48	67	..	38	54	28	93	..	..	98	90	92	87	93	51
12	Somalia	37x	50x	29x	18x	44x	5x	27x	50x	15x	48	23	23	35	..	78
13	Zambia	50	91	11	37	75	12	75x	100x	50x	100	85	88	88	42	90
14	Chad	24	48	17	..	..	..	30	64	..	43	18	18	23	..	15
15	Eritrea	..	..	7	..	..	7	..	..	..	46	36	36	27	21	68
16	Ethiopia	25	91	19	19	97	7	46	..	..	50	37	36	29	16	68
17	Mauritania	66x	67x	65x	..	34x	..	63	72	33	93	50	50	53	28	54
18	Bhutan	..	..	..	..	..	..	65	..	..	96	86	84	81	60	85
19	Nigeria	40	63	26	35	40	30	66	85	62	46	41	35	41	38	35
20	Zaire	27	37	23	23	46	11	26	40	17	43	29	29	33	25	46
21	Uganda	34	47	32	57	94	52	49	99	42	100	79	79	77	77	45
22	Cambodia	36	65	33	14	81	8	53	80	50	78	53	54	53	28	6
23	Burundi	70x	100x	69x	51	60	51	80	100	79	62	48	50	43	19	49
24	Central African Rep.	18	18	18	45	..	..	45	..	..	82	31	29	44	41	24
25	Burkina Faso	78	..	..	18	42	11	90	100	89	63	41	..	45	41	15
26	Madagascar	29	83	10	3	12	3	65	65	65	81	66	64	54	15	29
27	Tanzania, U. Rep. of	50	67	46	64	74	62	80	94	73	86	79	..	75	23	76
28	Lesotho	52	14	64	28	42	25	80	..	..	59	58	59	74	12	78
29	Gabon	68x	90x	50x	..	..	..	90x	..	..	97	66	66	65	..	25
30	Côte d'Ivoire	72	59	81	54	59	51	30x	61x	11x	49	44	44	49	..	15
31	Benin	50	41	53	20	54	6	18	..	..	90	81	81	75	85	77
32	Rwanda	66	75	62	58	77	56	80	..	..	32	23	23	25	..	47
33	Lao Peo. Dem. Rep.	45	57	43	27	97	14	67	..	..	69	48	57	73	34	55
34	Pakistan	79	96	71	33	62	19	55	99	35	78	66	66	65	30	59
35	Togo	63	74	58	23	56	10	61	90	60	73	71	71	58	72	33
36	Ghana	56	70	36	42	53	36	60	92	45	61	48	48	49	11	44
37	Haiti	28	37	23	24	42	16	50	..	..	42	41	40	24	12	20
38	Sudan	60	84	41	22	79	4	70	90	40	78	69	70	76	56	47
39	India	81	85	79	29	70	14	85	100	80	96	91	91	86	81	37
40	Nepal	46	90	43	21	70	16	..	..	..	61	63	62	57	11	49
41	Bangladesh	97	99	97	34	75	30	45	..	..	95	94	94	95	81	91
42	Senegal	52	85	28	58	83	40	40	..	..	71	55	55	49	32	18
43	Yemen	55	89	47	65	87	60	38	81	32	61	47	47	45	8	30
44	Indonesia	62	79	54	51	73	40	80	..	..	100	94	93	92	74	78
45	Bolivia	55	78	22	55	72	32	67	77	52	91	80	86	86	52	63
46	Cameroon	50	57	43	50	64	36	70	44	39	46	31	31	31	9	84
47	Congo	38x	92x	2x	..	..	..	83	97	70	94	79	79	70	..	67
48	Myanmar	38	36	39	36	39	35	60	100	47	83	77	77	77	68	37
49	Libyan Arab Jamahiriya	97x	100x	80x	98x	100x	85x	..	..	..	99	91	91	89	45	80
50	Papua New Guinea	28	84	17	22	82	11	96	..	..	91	66	66	39	13	51
51	Kenya	53	67	49	77	69	81	77	..	40	92	84	84	73	72	76
52	Turkmenistan	..	..	..	..	..	..	..	..	..	94	71	92	84	..	..
53	Tajikistan	..	..	..	..	..	..	..	..	..	69	82	74	97	..	..
54	Zimbabwe	77	99	64	66	99	48	85	96	80	90	80	80	77	..	82
55	Namibia	57	87	42	34	77	12	62	07	47	100	79	79	68	57	75
56	Mongolia	80	100	58	74	100	47	95	..	..	90	78	77	80	..	65
57	Iraq	44	..	..	70	85	37	93	97	78	90	67	67	98	60	70
58	Guatemala	62	92	43	60	72	52	34	47	25	70	71	73	66	11	24
59	South Africa	70	..	..	..	..	..	..	..	..	95	73	72	76	26	..
60	Nicaragua	58	81	23	60	77	34	83	100	60	89	74	84	74	..	40
61	Algeria	79	96	60	77	93	61	98	100	95	92	72	72	65	..	27
62	Uzbekistan	..	..	..	..	..	..	..	..	..	89	58	51	91	..	..
63	Brazil	87	..	..	83	..	..	..	..	..	92	73	68	76	..	63
64	Peru	71	88	28	57	58	25	75x	..	..	91	87	87	75	44	31
65	Philippines	85	93	77	69	79	62	76	77	74	89	86	88	87	69	63
66	Ecuador	71	82	55	48	56	38	88	70	20	100	80	78	100	..	70
67	El Salvador	55	78	38	81	91	65	40	80	40	83	92	92	81	79	45
68	Morocco	55	94	18	41	69	18	70	100	50	93	87	87	..	..	48
69	Kyrgyzstan	..	..	..	..	..	..	..	..	..	97	82	84	88	81	..
70	Turkey	80	91	59	..	..	..	..	..	..	72	81	81	76	29	57
71	Botswana	93x	100x	91x	55	91	41	89x	100x	85x	92	78	78	71	97	64
72	Honduras	65	81	53	75	96	61	64	80	56	95	95	95	94	88	70
73	Egypt	80	97	61	50	80	26	99	100	99	95	90	91	90	64	34
74	Azerbaijan	..	..	..	..	..	..	..	..	..	50	90	94	91	..	..
75	Iran, Islamic Rep. of	84	89	77	67	89	38	80	95	65	100	95	95	97	51	85

#	Country	% of population with access to safe water 1990-95			% of population with access to adequate sanitation 1990-95			% of population with access to health services 1985-95			% fully immunized 1990-94 1-year-old children				pregnant women tetanus	ORT use rate 1990-94
		total	urban	rural	total	urban	rural	total	urban	rural	TB	DPT	polio	measles		
76	Kazakhstan	..	..	..	..	..	..	..	..	..	87	80	75	72	..	..
77	Viet Nam	36	53	32	22	47	16	90	100	80	95	94	94	96	78	52
78	Dominican Rep.	76	96	46	78	76	83	80	84	67	64	83	98	87	85	37
79	China	67	97	56	24	74	7	92	100	89	94	93	94	89	3	84
80	Albania	..	..	..	..	..	..	..	..	..	81	96	97	81	92	..
81	Lebanon	94	96	88	63	81	8	95	98	85	..	..	95	73	..	45
82	Syrian Arab Rep.	85	92	78	83	84	82	90	96	84	100	89	89	84	51	95
83	Moldova	..	..	..	..	..	..	..	..	..	97	86	98	95	..	..
84	Saudi Arabia	95x	100x	74x	86x	100x	30x	97	100	88	94	93	94	92	63	90
85	Paraguay	35	50	24	62	56	67	63	90	38	97	84	83	79	43	52
86	Tunisia	99	100	89	96	98	94	90x	100x	80x	80	97	97	93	..	22
87	Thailand	86x	98x	87x	74	80	72	90	90	90	98	93	93	86	90	65
88	Armenia	..	..	..	..	..	..	..	..	..	83	83	92	95	..	..
89	TFYR Macedonia	..	..	..	..	..	..	..	..	..	96	88	91	86	91	..
90	Mexico	83	91	62	50	70	17	78	80	60	98	91	92	94	..	81
91	Russian Federation	..	..	..	..	..	..	..	..	..	87	65	82	88	..	..
92	Korea, Dem. Peo. Rep.	..	..	..	..	..	..	..	..	..	100	99	100	99	99	85
93	Romania	..	..	..	..	..	..	..	..	..	100	98	94	91	..	..
94	Georgia	..	..	..	..	..	..	..	..	..	67	58	69	16	..	..
95	Argentina	71	77	29	68	73	37	71	80	21	100	97	84	95	..	80
96	Oman	63	..	..	78	..	..	96	100	94	96	97	97	97	99	72
97	Latvia	..	..	..	..	..	..	..	..	..	89	70	72	81	..	..
98	Ukraine	..	..	..	..	..	..	..	..	..	89	90	91	94	..	..
99	Jordan	89	..	..	95	..	..	97	98	95	..	96	96	91	25	53
100	Venezuela	79	80	75	59	64	30	..	..	..	95	63	73	94	..	80
101	Estonia	..	..	..	..	..	..	..	..	..	99	79	87	76	..	..
102	Yugoslavia	..	..	..	..	..	..	..	..	..	68	85	83	85	..	..
103	Mauritius	99	95	100	99	99	99	100	100	100	87	89	89	85	78	..
104	Belarus	..	..	..	..	..	..	..	..	..	93	92	93	97	..	..
105	Uruguay	75x	85x	5x	61x	60x	65x	82	..	..	99	88	88	80	13	96
106	United Arab Emirates	95	..	..	77	93	22	99	..	..	98	90	90	90	..	81
107	Lithuania	..	..	..	..	..	..	..	..	..	96	83	88	93	..	..
108	Panama	83	..	..	88	99	73	80x	95x	64x	95	83	83	84	28	70
109	Trinidad and Tobago	97	99	91	79	99	98	100	100	99	..	85	85	79	..	75
110	Bulgaria	..	..	..	..	..	..	..	..	..	98	98	97	87	..	..
111	Sri Lanka	53	87	49	61	67	60	93x	..	..	86	88	88	84	79	76
112	Colombia	87	98	74	63	76	33	60	..	..	99	91	95	87	52	40
113	Bosnia and Herzegovina	..	..	..	..	..	..	..	..	..	24	38	45	48	..	..
114	Poland	..	..	..	..	..	..	..	..	..	95	95	95	95	..	..
115	Costa Rica	92	85	99	97	100	94	80x	100x	63x	97	88	88	88	..	78
116	Chile	85	94	37	83	84	5	97	..	..	96	92	92	96	..	90
117	Slovakia	..	..	..	..	..	..	..	..	..	91	98	98	97	..	..
118	Malaysia	78	96	66	94	..	..	..	..	..	97	90	90	81	..	47
119	Croatia	..	..	..	..	..	..	..	..	..	92	85	85	90	..	..
120	Hungary	..	..	..	..	..	..	..	..	..	100	99	99	99	..	..
121	Kuwait	..	..	..	..	100x	..	100	..	..	..	98	98	96	44	10
122	Jamaica	86	..	..	89	100	80	90	..	..	100	93	93	82	..	10
123	Portugal	..	..	..	..	..	..	..	..	..	92	92	92	94	..	..
124	Cuba	93	96	85	66	71	51	98	99	96	99	100	..	..	61	80
125	United States	..	..	..	..	..	..	..	..	..	..	88	79	84	..	..
126	Czech Rep.	..	..	..	..	..	..	..	..	..	98	98	98	97	..	..
127	Belgium	..	..	..	..	..	..	..	..	..	..	85	100	67	..	..
128	Greece	..	..	..	..	..	..	..	..	..	50	78	95	72	..	..
129	Spain	..	..	..	..	..	..	..	..	..	..	87	88	90	..	..
130	France	..	..	..	..	..	..	..	..	..	78	89	92	76	..	..
131	Israel	..	..	..	..	..	..	..	..	..	..	92	93	95	..	..
132	New Zealand	97	100	82	..	..	..	..	..	..	20	81	68	82	..	..
133	Korea, Rep. of	93	100	76	100	100	100	100	100	100	72	74	74	93	..	..
134	Slovenia	..	..	..	..	..	..	..	..	..	96	98	98	90	..	..
135	Australia	..	..	..	..	..	..	..	..	..	..	95	72	86	..	..
136	Italy	..	..	..	..	..	..	..	..	..	..	98	50	50	..	..
137	Netherlands	..	..	..	..	..	..	..	..	..	..	97	97	95	..	..
138	Norway	..	..	..	..	..	..	..	..	..	..	92	92	93	..	..
139	Canada	..	..	..	..	..	..	..	..	..	..	93	89	98	..	..
140	Austria	..	..	..	..	..	..	..	..	..	..	90	90	60	..	..
141	United Kingdom	..	..	..	..	..	..	..	..	..	..	91	93	92	..	..
142	Switzerland	..	..	..	..	..	..	..	..	..	..	89	95	83	..	..
143	Ireland	..	..	..	..	..	..	..	..	..	..	65	63	78	..	..
144	Germany	..	..	..	..	..	..	..	..	..	..	70	90	75	..	..
145	Denmark	..	..	..	..	..	..	..	..	..	..	88	95	81	..	..
146	Japan	97	100	85	..	85	..	..	..	..	93	87	94	69	..	..
147	Hong Kong	100	100	96	88	90	50	99x	..	..	99	83	81	77	..	..
148	Singapore	100x	100x	..	99x	99x	..	100	100	..	98	92	92	87	..	..
149	Finland	..	..	..	..	..	..	..	..	..	99	99	100	99	..	..
150	Sweden	..	..	..	..	..	..	..	..	..	..	99	99	95	..	..

Countries listed in descending order of their 1994 under-five mortality rates (table 1).

Table 4: Education

		Adult literacy rate				No. of sets per 1000 population 1992		Primary school enrolment ratio						% of primary school children reaching grade 5 1986-93	Secondary school enrolment ratio 1986-93 (gross)	
		1970		1990				1960 (gross)		1986-93 (gross)		1986-93 (net)				
		male	female	male	female	radio	television	male	female	male	female	male	female		male	female
1	Niger	8	1	18	5	61	5	8	3	37	21	31	19	82	9	4
2	Angola	16	7	56	29	29	6	30	14	95	87	..	..	34	..	..
3	Sierra Leone	18	5	40	14	224	10	30	15	56	39	..	..	..	21	12
4	Mozambique	34	10	52	19	47	3	71	43	69	51	47	37	35	9	5
5	Afghanistan	15	1	42	11	107	8	14	2	32	17	25	14	43	11	6
6	Guinea-Bissau	24	3	63	37	40	..	35	15	77	42	58	32	20	9	4
7	Guinea	25	6	45	18	42	7	27	9	57	27	34	17	80	17	6
8	Malawi	41	13	69	37	221	..	50	26	72	60	50	47	46	5	3
9	Liberia	29	5	49	18	226	18	40	13	51x	28x	..	..	..	31x	12x
10	Mali	13	1	33	17	44	1	13	5	32	19	17	14	76	10	5
11	Gambia	16	1	48	20	171	..	..	..	81	56	66	47	87	27	14
12	Somalia	8	1	36	14	38	12	6	2	15x	8x	11x	6x	..	9x	5x
13	Zambia	63	36	82	65	82	26	61	40	101	92	83	80	..	25	14
14	Chad	24	1	57	29	244	1	29	4	89	41	52	23	49	12	3
15	Eritrea	..	..	..	..	..	..	..	..	..	..	..	..	83	..	..
16	Ethiopia	9	1	41	21	187	3	9	3	26	18	33	24	22	11	10
17	Mauritania	..	..	47	24	144	23	12	3	70	55	..	..	72	20	10
18	Bhutan	..	..	51	23	16	..	5	..	31	19	..	..	..	7	2
19	Nigeria	39	10	61	39	173	33	54	31	85	67	..	..	87	21	26
20	Zaire	64	22	83	61	97	1	89	32	80	60	66	51	64	32x	13x
21	Uganda	53	15	70	44	109	10	39	18	78	64	58	51	55	16	18
22	Cambodia	74	23	48	22	112	8	..	..	..	..	..	..	..	..	..
23	Burundi	32	5	45	19	62	1	33	10	76	62	56	47	74	8	5
24	Central African Rep.	33	2	60	41	69	5	50	11	85	52	68	44	65	17	7
25	Burkina Faso	9	1	26	7	27	5	12	5	46	29	37	23	70	11	6
26	Madagascar	56	43	88	73	200	20	74	57	81	77	64	63	28	16	15
27	Tanzania, U. Rep. of	53	22	75	50	25	2	33	16	69	67	50	50	83	6	5
28	Lesotho	50	75	78	57	33	6	73	109	98	113	64	77	60	22	31
29	Gabon	52	34	68	45	143	37	..	..	..	..	..	..	50	..	..
30	Côte d'Ivoire	35	5	44	24	142	59	62	22	81	58	..	..	73	32	16
31	Benin	25	3	42	19	90	5	39	15	78	39	60	31	55	17	7
32	Rwanda	48	19	65	44	64	..	65	29	78	76	72	71	59	11	9
33	Lao Peo. Dem. Rep.	37	10	65	39	125	6	43	20	112	84	66	53	53	27	17
34	Pakistan	40	5	46	21	91	18	39	11	59	31	..	..	48	29	13
35	Togo	27	7	61	30	211	6	64	25	134	87	89	62	70	35	12
36	Ghana	43	18	71	46	269	16	58	31	80	67	..	..	80	48	29
37	Haiti	27	18	44	38	47	5	50	39	58	54	25	26	47	22	21
38	Sudan	27	2	53	28	250	77	29	11	58	45	..	..	94	23	19
39	India	47	19	62	34	80	37	83	44	113	90	..	..	62	60	37
40	Nepal	22	3	37	11	34	2	19	3	121	81	80	41	52	47	24
41	Bangladesh	47	9	47	23	44	5	80	31	83	71	74	64	47	25	12
42	Senegal	24	3	39	19	115	37	37	18	67	50	55	41	88	22	12
43	Yemen	14	3	53	26	28	28	..	..	111	43	..	..	..	47	10
44	Indonesia	68	43	88	75	147	60	78	58	116	113	99	95	86	47	39
45	Bolivia	62	41	88	71	613	103	70	43	89	81	85	78	60	37	31
46	Cameroon	51	18	70	44	146	24	77	37	109	93	82	71	66	32	23
47	Congo	56	27	78	59	114	6	..	..	..	..	..	..	72	..	..
48	Myanmar	78	47	88	75	82	2	60	53	107	104	..	..	..	23	23
49	Libyan Arab Jamahiriya	56	7	84	54	226	100	..	..	..	..	..	..	..	..	..
50	Papua New Guinea	39	24	78	57	73	3	24	15	78	66	78	66	69	15	10
51	Kenya	49	14	82	62	87	10	62	29	97	93	92x	89x	77	31	23
52	Turkmenistan	..	..	99x	97x	..	..	..	..	..	..	..	..	..	..	..
53	Tajikistan	..	..	99x	97x	..	..	..	..	..	..	..	..	..	..	..
54	Zimbabwe	63	47	88	77	84	27	82	65	123	114	..	..	76	53	41
55	Namibia	..	..	..	..	127	21	..	..	121	127	78	85	64	46	59
56	Mongolia	87	74	87	73	132	40	80	80	96	100	..	..	..	85x	97x
57	Iraq	48	13	66	38	216	73	94	36	96	82	82	73	72	52	33
58	Guatemala	50	35	61	46	66	52	48	39	84	73	..	..	..	20x	17x
59	South Africa	70	69	80	79	304	98	..	..	109	109	..	..	71	65	77
60	Nicaragua	57	57	63	65	262	66	57	59	100	104	79	82	55	40	45
61	Algeria	39	12	68	41	234	76	55	37	105	92	95	86	93	64	54
62	Uzbekistan	..	..	98x	96x	..	..	..	..	..	..	..	..	..	..	..
63	Brazil	69	63	82	80	386	208	58	56	101x	97x	..	..	72	31x	36x
64	Peru	82	60	93	80	254	98	98	74	125x	120x	..	..	..	66x	60x
65	Philippines	84	81	94	93	139	45	98	93	113	111	100	100	75	71	75
66	Ecuador	76	68	90	87	318	85	82	75	119	117	..	..	67	55	57
67	El Salvador	60	53	71	67	413	93	59	56	78	79	70	71	58	25	28
68	Morocco	33	9	52	26	210	74	69	28	80	57	69	50	80	40	29
69	Kyrgyzstan	..	..	98x	94x	..	..	..	..	..	..	..	..	..	..	..
70	Turkey	69	34	90	69	161	176	90	58	115	110	..	..	92	60	40
71	Botswana	28	27	78	55	122	17	38	43	114	118	94	99	84	51	57
72	Honduras	58	54	70	69	387	73	68	67	102	107	88	93	..	27	34
73	Egypt	57	30	61	34	328	119	79	52	110	93	..	..	98	88	71
74	Azerbaijan	..	..	99x	96x	..	..	..	..	..	..	..	..	..	..	..
75	Iran, Islamic Rep. of	46	13	72	52	232	63	59	28	114	104	100	93	89	70	54

| | | Adult literacy rate | | | | No. of sets per 1000 population 1992 | | Primary school enrolment ratio | | | | | | % of primary school children reaching grade 5 1986-93 | Secondary school enrolment ratio 1986-93 (gross) | |
| | | 1970 | | 1990 | | | | 1960 (gross) | | 1986-93 (gross) | | 1986-93 (net) | | | | |
		male	female	male	female	radio	television	male	female	male	female	male	female		male	female
76	Kazakhstan	..	..	99x	96x	..	..	..	..	..	..	..	..	..	..	..
77	Viet Nam	..	..	95	87	104	42	103	74	106x	100x	..	..	..	44x	41x
78	Dominican Rep.	69	66	80	80	171	87	75	74	95	96	73	73	..	44x	57x
79	China	..	..	87	68	182	31	131	90	125	116	99	94	88	59	48
80	Albania	..	..	..	..	176	88	102	86	100	101	..	..	98	84	74
81	Lebanon	79	58	94	88	835	324	112	105	113	109	..	..	..	67	71
82	Syrian Arab. Rep.	60	20	82	49	255	61	89	39	113	101	100	92	92	54	43
83	Moldova	..	..	99x	94x	..	..	..	..	..	..	..	..	..	..	..
84	Saudi Arabia	15	1	69	44	304	268	32	3	81	75	68	59	96	56	46
85	Paraguay	84	74	93	89	171	82	106	94	112	109	99	97	74	33	34
86	Tunisia	47	18	73	47	200	80	88	43	125	115	100	97	90	53	45
87	Thailand	87	70	96	91	192	114	97	88	92	88	..	..	88	34	32
88	Armenia	..	..	99x	98x	..	..	..	..	..	..	..	..	..	..	..
89	TFYR Macedonia	..	..	..	..	..	..	..	..	..	..	..	..	95	..	..
90	Mexico	78	70	90	85	255	149	80	75	114	111	..	..	84	56	56
91	Russian Federation	..	..	100x	98x	327	370	..	..	..	..	..	..	..	..	..
92	Korea, Dem. Peo. Rep.	..	..	..	..	122	18	..	..	108	100	..	..	..	..	..
93	Romania	98	93	99x	95x	199	196	101	95	88	87	79	77	93	82	82
94	Georgia	..	..	99x	98x	..	..	..	..	..	..	..	..	..	..	..
95	Argentina	94	92	96	96	683	221	99	99	108	115	..	..	..	67	74
96	Oman	..	..	..	..	637	730	..	..	104	96	86	83	96	68	61
97	Latvia	..	..	100x	99x	597	448	..	..	86	86	82	81	..	82	88
98	Ukraine	..	..	99x	97x	1177x	487x	..	..	..	..	..	..	..	..	..
99	Jordan	63	32	91	73	256	82	..	..	105	105	99	99	98	51	55
100	Venezuela	79	72	91	89	448	163	98	99	98	100	90	92	78	29	40
101	Estonia	..	..	100x	100x	449	351	..	..	85	85	81	81	93	88	94
102	Yugoslavia	..	..	..	..	..	..	..	..	..	..	..	..	..	..	..
103	Mauritius	83	68	85	75	360	218	96	90	104	108	87	90	100	52	56
104	Belarus	..	..	99x	97x	306x	268x	..	..	..	..	..	..	99	..	..
105	Uruguay	92	93	96	97	604	232	117	117	109	107	93	94	95	61x	62x
106	United Arab Emirates	24	7	77	76	326	111	..	..	119	117	100	100	99	69	76
107	Lithuania	..	..	99x	98x	380	375	..	..	93	91	..	..	94	77	80
108	Panama	79	78	89	88	224	167	89	86	108	105	91	92	82	59	64
109	Trinidad and Tobago	95	90	98	96	494	316	111	108	95	95	89	90	95	78	80
110	Bulgaria	96	90	..	..	445	257	94	92	91	88	81	80	88	68	72
111	Sri Lanka	86	68	93	85	200	49	107	95	109	105	..	..	92	71	78
112	Colombia	78	76	90	90	177	117	74	74	116	117	..	..	59	56	67
113	Bosnia and Herzegovina	..	..	..	..	..	..	..	..	..	..	..	..	..	..	..
114	Poland	99	97	99x	98x	435	295	110	107	99	97	96	96	98	82	86
115	Costa Rica	87	87	94	94	258	141	94	92	106	105	87	88	86	45	49
116	Chile	89	87	94	94	344	210	87	86	96	95	85	82	95	68	72
117	Slovakia	..	..	..	..	569	..	..	..	..	..	..	..	97	..	..
118	Malaysia	69	42	87	74	430	150	108	79	93	94	..	..	98	58	62
119	Croatia	..	..	..	..	..	..	..	..	..	..	..	..	100	..	..
120	Hungary	98	98	99x	98x	599	414	103	100	89	89	85	86	97	81	81
121	Kuwait	63	42	79	72	365	310	132	99	60	61	46	43	..	55	55
122	Jamaica	82	85	79	87	421	134	78	79	105	108	99	100	96	59	66
123	Portugal	78	65	89	81	229	188	132	129	121	118	100	100	..	65	97
124	Cuba	86	87	95	94	345	162	109	110	103	102	97	98	95	79	89
125	United States	99	99	..	..	2118	815	..	..	104	103	99	98	..	94	94
126	Czech Rep.	..	..	..	..	..	..	..	..	..	..	..	..	95	..	..
127	Belgium	99	99	..	..	769	453	111	108	98	100	94	96	..	102	103
128	Greece	93	76	98	89	421	201	104	101	97	98	93	94	99	99	97
129	Spain	94	86	97	93	312	402	106	116	107	107	100	100	96	104	113
130	France	99	98	..	..	889	408	144	143	107	105	100	100	94	100	104
131	Israel	93	83	95x	89x	471	271	99	97	94	94	..	..	100	83	89
132	New Zealand	..	..	..	..	931	443	110	106	104	103	100	100	94	91	92
133	Korea, Rep. of	94	81	99	95	1002	211	108	94	101	103	99	100	100	92	93
134	Slovenia	..	..	..	..	367	..	..	..	..	..	..	..	100	..	..
135	Australia	..	..	..	..	1273	482	103	103	107	107	98	98	99	82	84
136	Italy	95	92	98	96	791	421	112	109	94	97	..	..	..	77	77
137	Netherlands	..	..	..	..	907	488	105	104	96	99	93	96	..	119	114
138	Norway	..	..	..	..	795	424	100	100	99	99	99	99	100	112	109
139	Canada	..	..	..	..	1030	640	108	105	108	106	100	100	96	107	107
140	Austria	..	..	..	..	617	480	106	104	104	104	90	91	97	109	102
141	United Kingdom	..	..	..	..	1146	435	92	92	104	105	97	98	..	85	88
142	Switzerland	..	..	..	..	843	407	118	118	104	105	95	97	100	94	89
143	Ireland	..	..	..	..	637	304	107	112	103	103	90	91	100	99	107
144	Germany	..	..	..	..	885	558	..	..	93	94	89	90	..	98	96
145	Denmark	..	..	..	..	1033	537	103	103	95	95	95	95	100	109	111
146	Japan	100	99	..	..	908	614	103	102	102	102	100	100	100	96	98
147	Hong Kong	90	63	96	85	668	281	88	72	105x	104x	95x	95x	..	70x	75x
148	Singapore	83	54	95	83	646	379	120	101	110	107	100	100	100	70	71
149	Finland	..	..	..	..	997	505	100	95	100	99	..	..	100	113	135
150	Sweden	..	..	..	..	877	469	95	96	101	101	100	100	98	95	96

Countries listed in descending order of their 1994 under-five mortality rates (table 1).

Table 5: Demographic indicators

		Population (millions) 1994		Population annual growth rate (%)		Crude death rate		Crude birth rate		Life expectancy		Total fertility rate 1994	% of population urbanized 1994	Average annual growth rate of urban population (%)	
		under 16	under 5	1965-80	1980-94	1960	1994	1960	1994	1960	1994			1965-80	1980-94
1	Niger	4.5	1.8	2.8	3.3	29	19	54	53	36	46	7.3	17	6.8	5.4
2	Angola	5.3	2.1	2.0	3.0	31	19	49	51	34	46	7.0	32	5.5	5.9
3	Sierra Leone	2.0	0.8	1.9	2.2	33	25	48	49	32	39	6.4	36	5.0	4.8
4	Mozambique	7.3	2.8	2.5	1.8	26	19	47	45	38	46	6.4	33	9.5	8.4
5	Afghanistan	8.2	3.3	1.9	1.2	30	22	52	50	34	43	6.7	20	5.3	2.9
6	Guinea-Bissau	0.5	0.2	2.8	2.0	29	21	40	43	34	43	5.7	22	3.9	3.8
7	Guinea	3.2	1.3	1.6	2.7	31	20	53	51	34	44	6.9	29	4.9	5.7
8	Malawi	5.3	2.1	2.9	4.0	28	20	54	51	38	46	7.0	13	7.1	6.6
9	Liberia	1.4	0.6	3.0	3.2	25	14	50	47	42	55	6.7	45	6.1	4.9
10	Mali	5.2	2.1	2.2	3.0	29	19	52	51	35	46	7.0	26	4.8	5.6
11	Gambia	0.5	0.2	3.1	3.7	32	19	50	44	33	45	5.5	25	5.0	6.0
12	Somalia	4.5	1.8	3.1	2.2	28	19	50	50	37	47	6.9	26	3.9	3.2
13	Zambia	4.6	1.7	3.1	3.4	23	15	50	45	43	45	5.8	43	6.6	3.9
14	Chad	2.8	1.1	2.0	2.3	30	18	46	44	35	47	5.8	21	6.9	3.2
15	Eritrea	1.6	0.6	2.6	2.6	25	15	49	43	40	50	5.7	17	4.8	4.2
16	Ethiopia	25.9	10.3	2.4	2.7	28	18	51	49	37	47	6.9	13	4.5	4.4
17	Mauritania	1.0	0.4	2.3	2.6	26	15	46	40	39	51	5.3	53	10.1	6.8
18	Bhutan	0.7	0.3	1.9	1.9	26	15	42	40	38	50	5.7	6	4.1	5.3
19	Nigeria	51.8	20.1	2.6	2.9	24	16	52	45	40	50	6.3	39	5.7	5.5
20	Zaire	21.3	8.3	2.9	3.2	23	15	47	48	42	52	6.6	29	3.5	3.3
21	Uganda	10.5	4.2	3.3	3.2	21	19	50	52	44	45	7.1	12	5.3	5.6
22	Cambodia	4.6	1.8	0.4	3.1	21	15	45	44	43	51	5.1	20	1.3	6.5
23	Burundi	3.0	1.2	1.7	2.9	23	16	46	46	42	50	6.6	7	6.2	6.6
24	Central African Rep.	1.5	0.6	2.1	2.4	26	17	43	41	39	49	5.6	39	4.0	3.1
25	Burkina Faso	4.7	1.8	2.3	2.6	28	18	49	47	37	47	6.4	26	5.5	10.5
26	Madagascar	6.9	2.6	2.6	3.3	24	12	49	44	42	56	6.0	27	5.2	5.9
27	Tanzania, U. Rep. of	13.9	5.2	3.0	3.1	23	14	51	43	41	52	5.8	24	9.9	6.5
28	Lesotho	0.9	0.3	2.2	2.9	24	10	43	37	44	60	5.1	22	7.1	6.6
29	Gabon	0.5	0.2	3.3	3.3	24	16	31	37	41	53	5.4	49	6.7	5.6
30	Côte d'Ivoire	7.1	2.8	4.0	3.7	25	15	53	50	40	51	7.3	43	6.7	5.2
31	Benin	2.6	1.0	2.4	3.0	33	18	47	49	36	47	7.0	31	7.1	4.5
32	Rwanda	3.8	1.4	3.2	2.9	22	17	50	44	43	47	6.4	6	6.8	4.6
33	Lao Peo. Dem. Rep.	2.2	0.9	1.8	2.8	23	15	45	45	40	51	6.5	21	5.1	6.0
34	Pakistan	63.5	23.6	2.7	3.4	23	9	49	41	45	61	6.0	34	3.8	4.8
35	Togo	1.9	0.7	3.2	3.1	26	13	48	45	40	55	6.4	31	7.9	5.1
36	Ghana	8.1	3.0	2.1	3.3	19	12	48	42	46	56	5.8	36	3.3	4.3
37	Haiti	3.0	1.1	1.7	2.0	23	12	42	35	43	56	4.7	31	3.7	3.9
38	Sudan	12.7	4.6	2.8	2.7	25	13	47	40	40	53	5.6	24	5.6	4.1
39	India	344.5	116.6	2.2	2.1	21	10	43	29	45	60	3.7	27	3.6	3.1
40	Nepal	9.6	3.5	2.4	2.6	26	13	44	39	39	53	5.3	13	6.6	7.6
41	Bangladesh	49.9	17.1	2.8	2.1	22	12	47	36	40	55	4.2	18	6.7	5.3
42	Senegal	3.8	1.4	2.8	2.7	27	16	50	43	37	49	5.9	42	3.4	3.8
43	Yemen	6.8	2.7	2.3	3.7	28	16	53	49	37	50	7.5	33	6.3	7.2
44	Indonesia	69.4	21.9	2.3	1.8	23	9	44	25	42	62	2.8	35	4.6	5.0
45	Bolivia	3.1	1.1	2.4	2.2	22	10	46	36	43	59	4.7	60	3.2	4.1
46	Cameroon	6.0	2.2	2.6	2.8	24	12	44	41	40	56	5.6	44	6.9	5.3
47	Congo	1.2	0.5	2.7	2.9	23	15	45	45	42	51	6.2	58	4.3	5.4
48	Myanmar	18.0	6.4	2.2	2.1	21	11	42	33	45	57	4.1	26	3.1	2.7
49	Libyan Arab Jamahiriya	2.5	0.9	4.2	3.9	19	8	49	42	48	63	6.2	86	10.4	5.3
50	Papua New Guinea	1.8	0.6	2.4	2.2	23	11	44	34	42	56	4.9	16	8.6	3.6
51	Kenya	13.8	5.1	3.6	3.6	22	12	53	45	46	56	6.1	27	7.7	7.2
52	Turkmenistan	1.7	0.6	2.8	2.4	15	8	44	32	57	65	3.9	45	2.8	2.1
53	Tajikistan	2.7	1.0	3.0	2.9	13	6	47	37	60	70	4.8	32	2.9	2.5
54	Zimbabwe	5.1	1.9	3.1	3.1	20	12	53	39	46	54	4.9	32	6.0	5.6
55	Namibia	0.7	0.2	2.6	2.7	22	11	44	37	43	59	5.1	37	4.6	6.0
56	Mongolia	1.0	0.3	2.8	2.5	18	8	43	28	48	63	3.5	60	4.2	3.6
57	Iraq	9.2	3.3	3.3	3.0	20	7	49	38	50	66	5.6	74	5.0	3.9
58	Guatemala	4.8	1.8	2.8	2.9	19	8	49	39	47	65	5.2	41	3.4	3.5
59	South Africa	16.1	5.6	2.6	2.4	17	9	42	31	50	63	4.0	51	2.7	2.7
60	Nicaragua	2.1	0.8	3.1	3.0	19	7	51	41	48	66	4.9	62	4.6	4.1
61	Algeria	11.4	3.6	3.0	2.7	20	7	51	30	48	68	3.7	55	4.0	4.4
62	Uzbekistan	9.5	3.2	2.9	2.4	13	6	43	32	60	69	3.8	41	3.9	2.5
63	Brazil	55.4	17.8	2.4	1.9	13	8	43	25	56	66	2.8	78	4.3	3.1
64	Peru	8.8	2.9	2.7	2.1	19	7	47	28	49	66	3.3	72	4.2	2.9
65	Philippines	27.0	9.2	2.7	2.2	15	6	46	31	54	66	3.8	53	3.9	4.8
66	Ecuador	4.4	1.4	2.9	2.5	16	6	44	29	54	69	3.4	58	4.5	3.9
67	El Salvador	2.5	0.8	2.7	1.6	16	7	48	34	52	66	3.9	45	3.2	2.1
68	Morocco	10.3	3.4	2.5	2.2	21	8	50	29	48	63	3.6	48	4.2	3.3
69	Kyrgyzstan	1.8	0.6	2.2	1.8	14	7	38	29	59	69	3.6	39	2.7	1.9
70	Turkey	21.9	7.5	2.4	2.2	18	8	45	28	52	66	3.3	67	4.0	5.3
71	Botswana	0.7	0.2	3.3	3.3	20	7	52	37	47	65	4.7	27	12.5	7.5
72	Honduras	2.6	0.9	3.1	3.1	19	6	52	37	48	67	4.7	43	5.1	4.6
73	Egypt	25.0	8.1	2.2	2.4	21	8	45	30	47	63	3.7	45	2.7	2.6
74	Azerbaijan	2.5	0.8	2.0	1.4	10	6	40	23	65	70	2.4	56	2.5	1.7
75	Iran, Islamic Rep. of	30.4	10.4	3.1	3.7	21	7	47	36	51	67	4.9	58	4.9	4.9

		Population (millions) 1994		Population annual growth rate (%)		Crude death rate		Crude birth rate		Life expectancy		Total fertility rate 1994	% of population urbanized 1994	Average annual growth rate of urban population (%)	
		under 16	under 5	1965-80	1980-94	1960	1994	1960	1994	1960	1994			1965-80	1980-94
76	Kazakhstan	5.5	1.6	1.5	0.9	12	8	34	20	60	70	2.5	59	2.4	1.6
77	Viet Nam	29.1	10.1	2.2	2.2	23	8	41	31	45	65	3.8	21	3.3	2.7
78	Dominican Rep.	2.9	1.0	2.7	2.1	16	6	50	27	53	69	3.0	64	5.1	3.8
79	China	340.4	107.3	2.1	1.4	19	7	37	19	49	68	2.0	30	2.6	4.3
80	Albania	1.1	0.4	2.4	1.8	10	6	41	24	64	72	2.8	37	2.9	2.4
81	Lebanon	1.1	0.4	1.4	0.6	14	7	43	27	60	68	3.0	87	4.1	1.8
82	Syrian Arab Rep.	7.1	2.6	3.3	3.5	18	6	47	41	51	67	5.7	52	4.3	4.3
83	Moldova	1.3	0.4	1.2	0.7	13	10	26	17	62	68	2.1	51	3.7	2.4
84	Saudi Arabia	7.7	2.8	4.6	4.3	23	5	49	35	46	69	6.2	80	8.3	5.5
85	Paraguay	2.1	0.7	2.8	3.1	9	6	43	33	64	70	4.2	52	3.8	4.7
86	Tunisia	3.3	1.0	2.1	2.2	19	6	47	26	49	68	3.0	57	3.9	3.0
87	Thailand	18.0	5.4	2.8	1.6	15	6	44	20	54	69	2.1	20	4.7	2.6
88	Armenia	1.1	0.4	2.2	1.0	9	7	35	21	69	72	2.5	69	3.3	1.3
89	TFYR Macedonia	0.6	0.2	1.3	1.3	12	7	32	16	62	72	2.0	59	3.2	2.0
90	Mexico	35.4	11.8	2.9	2.2	13	5	45	28	58	71	3.1	75	4.2	3.1
91	Russian Federation	33.9	8.4	0.6	0.4	8	12	22	11	69	68	1.5	76	1.8	1.0
92	Korea, Dem. Peo. Rep.	7.2	2.6	2.6	1.8	13	5	42	24	55	71	2.3	61	4.1	2.3
93	Romania	5.2	1.3	1.0	0.2	9	11	20	12	67	70	1.5	55	2.8	1.0
94	Georgia	1.4	0.4	0.8	0.5	12	9	25	16	65	73	2.1	58	1.7	1.4
95	Argentina	10.6	3.3	1.5	1.4	9	8	24	21	65	72	2.7	88	2.1	1.8
96	Oman	1.0	0.4	3.7	4.5	28	5	51	44	41	69	7.0	13	7.6	8.2
97	Latvia	0.6	0.2	0.7	0.1	10	13	16	12	70	69	1.6	72	1.7	0.6
98	Ukraine	11.2	3.0	0.6	0.2	9	13	19	12	71	70	1.6	70	1.9	1.1
99	Jordan	2.4	0.9	2.7	4.1	23	6	50	39	48	68	5.4	71	4.4	5.3
100	Venezuela	8.3	2.8	3.4	2.5	10	5	45	28	61	72	3.2	92	4.6	3.2
101	Estonia	0.3	0.1	0.9	0.3	11	13	16	11	70	69	1.6	73	1.8	0.6
102	Yugoslavia	2.6	0.7	0.8	0.9	11	10	22	14	64	72	2.0	56	3.0	2.2
103	Mauritius	0.3	0.1	1.7	1.0	10	7	44	21	60	70	2.3	41	2.6	0.7
104	Belarus	2.4	0.6	0.7	0.4	10	12	23	12	69	70	1.7	70	3.4	1.9
105	Uruguay	0.8	0.3	0.5	0.6	10	10	22	17	68	72	2.3	90	0.9	1.0
106	United Arab Emirates	0.6	0.2	13.0	4.3	19	3	46	24	55	74	4.1	83	15.6	5.4
107	Lithuania	0.9	0.3	1.0	0.5	8	11	21	14	70	71	1.8	71	3.1	1.6
108	Panama	0.9	0.3	2.7	2.0	10	5	40	25	62	73	2.8	53	3.4	2.5
109	Trinidad and Tobago	0.5	0.1	1.3	1.3	9	6	38	21	64	71	2.4	71	1.2	2.1
110	Bulgaria	1.8	0.5	0.5	0.0	9	13	18	11	70	71	1.5	70	2.4	0.9
111	Sri Lanka	6.0	1.8	1.9	1.4	9	6	36	21	63	72	2.4	22	2.4	1.6
112	Colombia	12.3	3.9	2.4	1.9	12	6	45	24	58	69	2.6	72	3.6	2.8
113	Bosnia and Herzegovina	0.9	0.2	0.9	-0.7	10	7	33	14	62	72	1.6	49	3.9	1.6
114	Poland	9.6	2.5	0.8	0.5	8	10	24	13	68	71	1.9	64	1.8	1.2
115	Costa Rica	1.3	0.4	2.9	2.7	10	4	47	27	63	76	3.1	49	3.7	3.7
116	Chile	4.4	1.5	1.8	1.7	13	6	38	22	58	74	2.5	84	2.6	1.9
117	Slovakia	1.3	0.4	0.9	0.5	8	11	22	15	70	71	1.9	58	3.1	1.4
118	Malaysia	7.9	2.7	2.5	2.6	15	5	44	29	55	71	3.5	53	4.7	4.2
119	Croatia	0.9	0.3	0.4	0.2	11	12	19	11	67	71	1.7	63	2.8	1.9
120	Hungary	2.0	0.6	0.4	-0.4	10	15	16	12	68	69	1.7	64	1.8	0.5
121	Kuwait	0.7	0.2	7.1	1.2	10	2	44	25	61	75	3.0	99	8.1	1.9
122	Jamaica	0.8	0.3	1.3	0.9	9	6	39	22	64	73	2.3	53	2.7	1.9
123	Portugal	2.0	0.6	0.4	0.0	11	10	24	12	64	75	1.6	35	1.8	1.3
124	Cuba	2.6	0.9	1.5	0.9	9	7	31	17	65	75	1.8	76	2.6	1.6
125	United States	60.9	20.2	1.1	1.0	9	9	23	16	70	76	2.1	76	1.2	1.2
126	Czech Rep.	2.2	0.7	0.4	0.0	11	13	15	13	70	71	1.8	65	2.1	0.2
127	Belgium	1.9	0.6	0.3	0.2	12	11	17	12	71	76	1.7	97	0.4	0.3
128	Greece	1.9	0.5	0.8	0.6	8	10	19	10	69	78	1.4	65	2.1	1.4
129	Spain	7.0	1.9	1.1	0.4	9	9	21	10	70	70	1.2	70	2.2	0.7
130	France	12.2	3.7	0.7	0.5	12	10	18	13	71	77	1.7	73	1.3	0.4
131	Israel	1.7	0.6	2.8	2.4	6	7	27	21	69	76	2.8	90	3.4	2.6
132	New Zealand	0.9	0.3	1.1	0.9	9	8	26	17	71	75	2.1	86	1.5	1.1
133	Korea, Rep. of	11.5	3.5	1.9	1.1	14	6	43	16	55	71	1.8	80	5.7	3.5
134	Slovenia	0.4	0.1	0.8	0.4	10	11	18	11	69	73	1.5	63	3.4	2.3
135	Australia	4.1	1.3	1.6	1.5	9	7	22	15	71	77	1.9	85	1.9	1.4
136	Italy	9.5	2.8	0.5	0.1	10	10	18	10	70	77	1.3	67	1.0	0.1
137	Netherlands	3.0	1.0	0.9	0.6	8	9	21	13	73	77	1.6	89	1.2	0.6
138	Norway	0.9	0.3	0.6	0.4	9	11	18	14	73	77	2.0	73	2.0	0.6
139	Canada	6.5	2.1	1.5	1.2	8	8	26	15	71	77	1.9	77	1.7	1.3
140	Austria	1.5	0.5	0.3	0.3	13	11	18	12	69	76	1.6	56	0.8	0.4
141	United Kingdom	12.0	3.9	0.2	0.2	12	11	17	14	71	76	1.8	89	0.4	0.3
142	Switzerland	1.3	0.4	0.5	0.9	10	9	18	13	72	78	1.6	61	1.0	1.3
143	Ireland	1.0	0.3	1.1	0.3	12	9	21	15	70	75	2.1	57	2.0	0.6
144	Germany	14.0	4.1	0.2	0.3	12	12	17	10	70	76	1.3	86	0.6	0.6
145	Denmark	0.9	0.3	0.5	0.1	9	12	17	12	72	75	1.7	85	1.0	0.2
146	Japan	22.4	6.2	1.1	0.5	8	7	18	10	69	79	1.5	78	1.9	0.6
147	Hong Kong	1.2	0.3	2.1	1.1	7	6	35	11	67	79	1.2	95	2.5	1.3
148	Singapore	0.7	0.2	1.7	1.1	8	6	38	16	66	75	1.7	100	1.7	1.1
149	Finland	1.0	0.3	0.3	0.4	9	10	19	13	69	76	1.9	63	2.4	0.8
150	Sweden	1.7	0.6	0.5	0.4	10	11	15	14	73	78	2.1	83	1.0	0.4

Countries listed in descending order of their 1994 under-five mortality rates (table 1).

Table 6: Economic indicators

		GNP per capita (US$) 1993	GNP per capita average annual growth rate (%) 1965-80	GNP per capita average annual growth rate (%) 1980-93	Rate of inflation (%) 1980-93	% of population below absolute poverty level 1980-89 urban	% of population below absolute poverty level 1980-89 rural	% of central government expenditure allocated to 1986-93 health	education	defence	ODA inflow in millions US$ 1993	ODA inflow as a % of recipient GNP 1993	Debt service as a % of exports of goods and services 1970	1993
1	Niger	270	-2.5	-4.1	1	..	35x	..	..	..	334	14	3	17
2	Angola	700	..	-0.9x	6x	..	..	6	15	34	300	9	..	3
3	Sierra Leone	150	0.7	-1.5	62	..	65x	10	13	10	192	28	11	2
4	Mozambique	90	..	-1.5	42	50	67	5	10	35	1155	85	..	17
5	Afghanistan	280x	0.6	..	..	18x	36x	..	..	..	214	4	..	..
6	Guinea-Bissau	240	-2.7	2.8	59	..	..	1	3	4	98	41	..	8
7	Guinea	500	1.3	1.3x	20x	..	85	3	11	29	420	13	..	12
8	Malawi	200	3.2	-1.2	16	25	85	7	12	5	504	24	7	20
9	Liberia	450x	0.5	5.2x	..	..	23x	5	11	9	121	12	8	..
10	Mali	270	2.1x	-1.0	4	27x	48x	2	9	8	362	13	2	3
11	Gambia	350	..	-0.2	16	..	..	7	11	4	96	27	0	11
12	Somalia	120x	-0.1	-2.3x	75x	40x	70x	1	2	38	881	106	2	0
13	Zambia	380	-1.2	-3.1	59	25	..	7	9	..	811	24	6	20
14	Chad	210	-1.9	3.2	1	30x	56x	8	8	..	230	18	4	6
15	Eritrea	100	..	..	..	..	..	..	..	..	67	2	..	..
16	Ethiopia	100	0.4	-1.8x	5x	60	65	3	10	39	1209	23	11	8
17	Mauritania	500	-0.1	-0.8	8	..	..	4	23	..	331	30	4	25
18	Bhutan	170	..	4.5x	9x	..	..	5	11	..	67	25x	..	8
19	Nigeria	300	4.2	-0.1	21	..	..	1	3	3	206	1	4	14
20	Zaire	220x	-1.3	-0.8x	61x	..	80x	0	0	27	191	2	5	1
21	Uganda	180	-2.2	1.9x	79x	..	..	2	15	26	707	22	3	115
22	Cambodia	200x	..	..	..	..	..	..	..	..	313	27	..	0
23	Burundi	180	2.4	0.9	5	55x	85x	4	16	16	276	26	4	35
24	Central African Rep.	400	0.8	-1.6	4	..	91	..	..	..	180	14	5	3
25	Burkina Faso	300	1.7	0.8	3	..	..	5	14	18	426	14	4	7
26	Madagascar	220	-0.4	-2.6	16	50x	50x	7	17	8	369	12	4	11
27	Tanzania, U. Rep. of	90	0.8	0.1	24	..	..	6x	8x	16x	978	39	1	23
28	Lesotho	650	6.8	-0.5	14	50x	55x	12	22	7	132	11	3	6
29	Gabon	4960	5.6	-1.6	2	..	..	..	..	..	102	2	6	2
30	Côte d'Ivoire	630	2.8	-4.6	2	30	26	4	..	..	840	10	7	14
31	Benin	430	-0.3	-0.4	1	..	..	6	31	17	258	12	3	7
32	Rwanda	210	1.6	-1.2	3	30	90x	5	26	..	394	25	0	5
33	Lao Peo. Dem. Rep.	280	..	2.1x	27x	..	..	..	..	..	198	15	..	9
34	Pakistan	430	1.8	3.1	7	32x	29x	1	2	28	1067	2	22	19
35	Togo	340	1.7	-2.1	4	42x	..	5	20	11	125	9	3	4
36	Ghana	430	-0.8	0.1	37	59	37	7	22	5	624	9	5	14
37	Haiti	370x	0.9	-3.4x	8x	65	80	..	..	..	128	5	6	0
38	Sudan	480x	0.8	-0.2x	55x	..	85x	..	..	13x	485	8	10	3
39	India	300	1.5	3.0	9	29	33	2	2	15	1533	1	21	25
40	Nepal	190	..	2.0	12	55x	61x	5	11	6	360	9	3	11
41	Bangladesh	220	-0.3	2.1	9	86x	86x	5	11	10	1359	5	0	11
42	Senegal	750	-0.5	0.0	5	..	..	..	..	..	496	8	4	5
43	Yemen	520x	..	..	..	..	..	4	19	30	336	5	..	6
44	Indonesia	740	5.2	4.2	9	20	16	3	10	6	2024	1	7	20
45	Bolivia	760	1.7	-0.7	187	..	..	7	11	8	570	11	11	50
46	Cameroon	820	2.4	-2.2	4	15x	40x	3	12	7	643	6	3	14
47	Congo	950	2.7	-0.3	-1	..	..	..	..	..	133	6	11	8
48	Myanmar	220x	1.6	2.1x	17	40x	40x	7	17	33	102	..	18	16
49	Libyan Arab Jamahiriya	5310x	0.0	-9.2x	0x	..	..	..	..	..	6	0	..	..
50	Papua New Guinea	1130	..	0.6	5	10x	75x	8	15	4	359	8	1	10
51	Kenya	270	3.1	0.3	10	10x	55x	5	19	6	929	14	6	18
52	Turkmenistan	1230x	..	-1.6x	17	..	..	..	..	..	10	0	..	..
53	Tajikistan	470	..	-3.6	26	..	..	..	..	..	23	1	..	..
54	Zimbabwe	520	1.7	-0.3	14	..	..	8	24	17	428	8	2	25
55	Namibia	1820	..	0.7	12	..	..	10	22	7	166	6	..	..
56	Mongolia	390	..	0.2	14	..	..	1	2	12	112	12	..	4
57	Iraq	1036x	..	..	..	..	..	..	..	..	170	1	..	..
58	Guatemala	1100	3.0	-1.2	17	17	51	10	20	13	202	2	7	11
59	South Africa	2980	3.2	-0.2	15	..	..	13	14	7	..	..	..	..
60	Nicaragua	340	-0.7	-5.7	665	21x	19x	13	14	7	337	24	11	28
61	Algeria	1780	4.2	-0.8	13	20x	..	..	..	..	332	1	3	73
62	Uzbekistan	970	..	-0.2	25	..	..	..	..	..	5	0	..	..
63	Brazil	2930	6.3	0.3	423	9	34	5	4	3	234	0	12	11
64	Peru	1490	0.8	-2.7	316	46	83	5	16	11	560	2	12	39
65	Philippines	850	3.2	-0.6	14	52	64	4	15	10	1485	3	8	22
66	Ecuador	1200	5.4	0.0	40	40	65	11	18	13	237	2	8	21
67	El Salvador	1320	1.5	0.2	17	20	32	7	13	16	382	5	4	15
68	Morocco	1040	2.7	1.2	7	28x	45x	3	18	13	605	2	8	28
69	Kyrgyzstan	850	..	0.1	29	..	..	..	..	..	46	1	..	0
70	Turkey	2970	3.6	2.4	54	..	..	4	20	11	460	0	16	23
71	Botswana	2790	9.9	6.2	12	40	55	5	21	13	112	3	2	4
72	Honduras	600	1.1	-0.3	8	31	70	10	19	7	314	10	3	29
73	Egypt	660	2.8	2.8	14	34	34	2	10	8	2256	6	27	13
74	Azerbaijan	730	..	-3.5	28	..	..	..	..	..	14	0	..	..
75	Iran, Islamic Rep. of	2200x	2.9	-0.7x	17	..	..	7	19	7	139	1	..	3

		GNP per capita (US$) 1993	GNP per capita average annual growth rate (%)		Rate of inflation (%) 1980-93	% of population below absolute poverty level 1980-89		% of central government expenditure allocated to 1986-93			ODA inflow in millions US$ 1993	ODA inflow as a % of recipient GNP 1993	Debt service as a % of exports of goods and services	
			1965-80	1980-93		urban	rural	health	education	defence			1970	1993
76	Kazakhstan	1560	..	-1.6	35	..	..	..	..	..	10	0	..	0
77	Viet Nam	170	..	4.8x	119x	..	..	..	..	..	322	3	..	9
78	Dominican Rep.	1230	3.8	0.7	25	45x	43x	14	10	5	-1	0	4	11
79	China	490	4.1	8.2	7	..	13	0	2	16	3280	1	0x	10
80	Albania	340	..	-3.2	6	..	..	..	..	..	275	24	..	0
81	Lebanon	2150x	..	..	..	..	..	..	..	..	132	5	..	3
82	Syrian Arab Rep.	1160x	5.1	-2.1x	22x	..	..	2	9	39	168	1	11	3
83	Moldova	1060	..	-2.0	32	..	..	..	..	..	..	..	..	0
84	Saudi Arabia	7510x	4.0x	-3.6	-2	..	..	6	14	36	30	0	..	..
85	Paraguay	1510	4.1	-0.7	25	19x	50x	7	22	11	133	2	12	14
86	Tunisia	1720	4.7	1.2	7	20x	15x	6	18	6	236	2	18	18
87	Thailand	2110	4.4	6.4	4	10	25	8	21	17	615	1	3	4
88	Armenia	660	..	-4.2	27	..	..	..	..	..	35	1	..	1
89	TFYR Macedonia	820	..	..	..	..	..	..	..	..	..	..	..	..
90	Mexico	3610	3.6	-0.5	58	..	..	2	12	2	399	0	24	16
91	Russian Federation	2340	..	-1.0	35	..	..	..	..	..	..	..	..	4
92	Korea, Dem. Peo. Rep.	970x	..	..	..	..	..	..	..	..	15	..	..	..
93	Romania	1140	..	-2.4	22	..	..	9	10	10	..	..	0x	4
94	Georgia	580	..	-6.6	41	..	..	..	..	..	28	1	..	3
95	Argentina	7220	1.7	-0.5	374	..	..	3	10	10	279	0	22	39
96	Oman	4850	9.0	3.4	-2	..	..	6	13	35	77	1	..	10
97	Latvia	2010	..	-0.6	24	..	..	..	..	..	..	..	..	1
98	Ukraine	2210	..	0.2	37	..	..	..	..	..	..	..	..	..
99	Jordan	1190	5.8x	-5.9x	7x	14x	17x	6	14	22	317	7	4	13
100	Venezuela	2840	2.3	-0.7	24	..	..	10	20	6	49	0	3	13
101	Estonia	3080	..	-2.2	30	..	..	18	9	3	..	..	..	2
102	Yugoslavia	a	..	..	..	..	..	..	..	..	..	..	..	..
103	Mauritius	3030	3.7	5.5	9	12x	12x	9	15	2	39	1	3	5
104	Belarus	2870	..	2.4	31	..	..	3	18	4	..	..	..	1
105	Uruguay	3830	2.5	-0.1	67	22	..	6	7	8	121	1	22	38
106	United Arab Emirates	21430	..	-4.4	1x	..	..	7	17	38	-9	0	..	..
107	Lithuania	1320	..	-2.8	35	..	..	5	7	4	..	..	..	..
108	Panama	2600	2.8	-0.7	2	21x	30x	25	16	4	79	1	8	9
109	Trinidad and Tobago	3830	3.1	-2.8	5	..	39x	..	..	..	7	0	5	20
110	Bulgaria	1140	..	0.5	16	..	..	3	3	6	..	..	..	5
111	Sri Lanka	600	2.8	2.7	11	..	..	5	10	11	553	5	11	9
112	Colombia	1400	3.7	1.5	25	32	70	4	25	9	101	0	12	25
113	Bosnia and Herzegovina	b	..	..	..	..	..	..	..	..	..	..	..	..
114	Poland	2260	..	0.4	69	..	..	..	..	..	..	..	..	8
115	Costa Rica	2150	3.3	1.1	22	8	20	29	22	2	98	1	10	15
116	Chile	3170	0.0	3.6	20	12	20	12	13	9	177	0	19	13
117	Slovakia	1950	..	..	..	..	..	..	..	..	..	..	..	7
118	Malaysia	3140	4.7	3.5	2	13	38	6	20	12	101	0	4	6
119	Croatia	a	..	..	..	..	..	17	5	21	..	..	..	..
120	Hungary	3350	5.1	1.2	13	..	..	8	3	4	..	..	..	36
121	Kuwait	19360	0.6x	-4.3	-3x	..	..	6	10	20	3	0	..	..
122	Jamaica	1440	-0.1	-0.3	22	..	80	7	11	8	111	3	3	15
123	Portugal	9130	4.6	3.3	16	..	..	8	12	5	..	..	7	16
124	Cuba	1170x	..	..	..	..	..	23	10	..	31	0	..	..
125	United States	24740	1.8	1.7	4	..	..	17	2	19	..	..	..	..
126	Czech Rep.	2710	..	-2.0x	11x	..	..	..	..	..	..	..	..	7
127	Belgium	21650	3.6	1.9	4	..	..	2	12	5	..	..	..	..
128	Greece	7390	4.8	0.9	17	..	..	7	9	9	44	0	9	..
129	Spain	13590	4.1	2.7	8	..	..	6	5	4	..	..	..	..
130	France	22490	3.7	1.6	5	..	..	16	7	6	..	..	..	..
131	Israel	13920	3.7	2.0	70	..	..	4	12	20	1272	2	3	..
132	New Zealand	12600	1.7	0.7	9	..	..	12	14	4	..	..	..	..
133	Korea, Rep. of	7660	7.3	8.2	6	18x	11x	1	17	20	-35	0	20	6
134	Slovenia	6490	..	..	..	..	..	..	..	..	..	..	..	..
135	Australia	17500	2.2	1.6	6	..	..	13	7	8	..	..	..	..
136	Italy	19840	3.2	2.1	9	..	..	10	7	3	..	..	..	..
137	Netherlands	20950	2.7	1.7	2	..	..	14	10	4	..	..	..	..
138	Norway	25970	3.6	2.2	5	..	..	10	9	8	..	..	..	..
139	Canada	19970	3.3	1.4	4	..	..	5	3	7	..	..	..	..
140	Austria	23510	4.0	2.0	4	..	..	13	10	2	..	..	..	..
141	United Kingdom	18060	2.0	2.3	6	..	..	14	3	10	..	..	..	..
142	Switzerland	35760	1.5	1.1	4	..	..	13x	3x	10x	..	..	..	..
143	Ireland	13000	2.8	3.6	5	..	..	14	12	3	..	..	..	..
144	Germany	23560	3.0x	2.1	3	..	..	18	1	8	..	..	..	..
145	Denmark	26730	2.2	2.0	5	..	..	1	10	5	..	..	..	..
146	Japan	31490	5.1	3.4	2	..	..	..	..	..	..	..	..	..
147	Hong Kong	18060	6.2	5.4	8	..	..	8	17	..	33	0	..	..
148	Singapore	19850	8.3	6.1	3	..	..	6	22	25	23	0	1	..
149	Finland	19300	3.6	1.5	6	..	..	11	13	4	..	..	..	..
150	Sweden	24740	2.0	1.3	7	..	..	1	7	5	..	..	..	..

Countries listed in descending order of their 1994 under-five mortality rates (table 1).
a: Range US$696 to US$2785.   b: Range US$695 or less.

Table 7: Women

		Life expectancy females as a % of males 1994	Adult literacy rate females as a % of males 1990	Enrolment ratios females as a % of males 1986-93		Contraceptive prevalence (%) 1980-94	% of pregnant women immunized against tetanus 1990-94	% of births attended by trained health personnel 1983-94	Maternal mortality rate 1980-92
				primary school	secondary school				
1	Niger	107	28	57	44	4	44	15	590
2	Angola	107	52	92	..	1x	18	15	..
3	Sierra Leone	108	35	70	57	4	61	25	450
4	Mozambique	107	37	74	56	4	37	25	300
5	Afghanistan	102	26	53	55	2x	6	9	640
6	Guinea-Bissau	107	59	55	44	1x	55	27	700
7	Guinea	102	40	47	35	1x	56	36	800
8	Malawi	102	54	83	60	13	76	55	620
9	Liberia	106	37	55x	39x	6	35	58	..
10	Mali	107	52	59	50	5	6	32	2000
11	Gambia	107	42	69	52	..	93	80	1050
12	Somalia	107	39	53x	56x	1	..	2	1100
13	Zambia	104	79	91	56	15	42	51	150
14	Chad	107	51	46	25	1x	..	15	960
15	Eritrea	106	..	..	..	..	21	..	..
16	Ethiopia	107	51	69	91	2	16	14	560
17	Mauritania	106	51	79	50	4	28	40	..
18	Bhutan	106	45	61	29	2	60	7	620
19	Nigeria	106	64	79	124	6	38	37	800
20	Zaire	108	73	75	41x	1x	25	..	800
21	Uganda	105	63	82	113	5	77	38	550
22	Cambodia	106	46	..	..	..	28	47	500
23	Burundi	108	42	82	63	9	19	19	..
24	Central African Rep.	111	68	61	41	15	41	46	600
25	Burkina Faso	107	27	63	55	8	41	42	810
26	Madagascar	105	83	95	94	17	15	56	660
27	Tanzania, U. Rep. of	106	67	97	83	18	23	53	340
28	Lesotho	109	73	115	141	23	12	40	..
29	Gabon	106	66	..	..	..	..	80	190
30	Côte d'Ivoire	106	55	72	50	11	..	45	..
31	Benin	107	45	50	41	9	85	45	160
32	Rwanda	107	68	97	82	21	..	26	210
33	Lao Peo. Dem. Rep.	106	60	75	63	..	34	..	300
34	Pakistan	103	46	53	45	12	30	35	500
35	Togo	108	49	65	34	12	72	54	420
36	Ghana	107	65	84	60	20	11	59	390
37	Haiti	105	86	93	95	18	12	20	600
38	Sudan	106	53	78	83	9	56	69	550
39	India	100	55	80	62	43	81	33	460
40	Nepal	98	30	67	51	23	11	6	520
41	Bangladesh	100	49	86	48	45	81	10	600
42	Senegal	104	49	75	55	7	32	46	560
43	Yemen	100	49	39	21	7	8	16	..
44	Indonesia	105	85	97	83	55	74	36	450
45	Bolivia	107	81	91	84	45	52	47	390
46	Cameroon	106	63	85	72	16	9	64	430
47	Congo	110	76	..	..	..	..	..	900
48	Myanmar	105	85	97	100	13	68	57	460
49	Libyan Arab Jamahiriya	107	64	..	..	..	45	76	70
50	Papua New Guinea	104	73	85	67	4	13	20	900
51	Kenya	107	76	96	74	33	72	54	170x
52	Turkmenistan	111	98x	..	..	..	..	..	..
53	Tajikistan	109	98x	..	..	..	..	..	..
54	Zimbabwe	104	88	93	77	43	..	70	400
55	Namibia	105	..	105	128	29	57	68	230
56	Mongolia	105	84	104	114x	..	60	99	240
57	Iraq	105	58	85	63	18	60	50	120
58	Guatemala	108	75	87	85x	23	11	51	200
59	South Africa	110	99	100	118	50	26	..	84
60	Nicaragua	106	103	104	113	49	..	73	..
61	Algeria	103	60	88	84	51	..	15	140x
62	Uzbekistan	109	98x	..	..	..	..	..	..
63	Brazil	108	98	96x	116x	66	..	95	200
64	Peru	106	86	96x	91x	59	44	52	200
65	Philippines	106	99	98	106	40	69	53	210
66	Ecuador	108	97	98	104	53	..	84	170
67	El Salvador	110	94	101	112	53	79	66	160
68	Morocco	107	50	71	73	42	..	31	330
69	Kyrgyzstan	112	96x	..	..	..	81	..	..
70	Turkey	106	77	96	67	63	29	76	150
71	Botswana	105	71	104	112	33	97	78	250
72	Honduras	108	99	105	126	47	88	81	220
73	Egypt	105	56	85	81	47	64	41	270
74	Azerbaijan	112	97x	..	..	..	..	..	..
75	Iran, Islamic Rep. of	101	72	91	77	49	51	70	120

		Life expectancy females as a % of males 1994	Adult literacy rate females as a % of males 1990	Enrolment ratios females as a % of males 1986-93		Contraceptive prevalence (%) 1980-94	% of pregnant women immunized against tetanus 1990-94	% of births attended by trained health personnel 1983-94	Maternal mortality rate 1980-92
				primary school	secondary school				
76	Kazakhstan	114	97x	..	..	..	..	..	..
77	Viet Nam	106	92	94x	93x	53	78	95	120
78	Dominican Rep.	107	100	101	130x	56	85	92	..
79	China	104	78	93	81	83	3	94	95
80	Albania	109	..	101	88	..	92	99	..
81	Lebanon	106	94	96	106	55x	..	45x	..
82	Syrian Arab Rep.	106	60	89	80	52	51	61	140
83	Moldova	113	95x	..	..	..	..	..	..
84	Saudi Arabia	104	64	93	82	..	63	90	41
85	Paraguay	106	96	97	103	48	43	66	300
86	Tunisia	101	64	92	85	50	..	69	70
87	Thailand	109	95	96	94	66	90	71	50
88	Armenia	109	99x	..	..	..	..	..	..
89	TFYR Macedonia	109	..	..	..	..	91	..	..
90	Mexico	109	94	97	100	53	..	77	110
91	Russian Federation	119	98x	..	..	..	..	..	..
92	Korea, Dem. Peo. Rep.	109	..	93	..	..	99	100	41
93	Romania	109	96x	99	100	57	..	100x	72
94	Georgia	113	99x	..	..	..	..	..	..
95	Argentina	110	100	106	110	74	..	87x	140
96	Oman	106	..	92	90	9	99	60	..
97	Latvia	117	99x	100	107	..	..	..	..
98	Ukraine	116	98x	..	..	..	..	..	..
99	Jordan	106	80	100	108	35	25	87	48x
100	Venezuela	109	98	102	138	49x	..	69	..
101	Estonia	117	100x	100	107	..	..	..	..
102	Yugoslavia	107	..	..	..	..	..	..	..
103	Mauritius	110	88	104	108	75	78	85	99
104	Belarus	115	98x	..	..	..	..	..	..
105	Uruguay	110	101	98	102x	..	13	96	36
106	United Arab Emirates	103	99	98	110	..	..	99	..
107	Lithuania	117	99x	98	104	..	..	..	..
108	Panama	106	99	97	108	58	28	96	75
109	Trinidad and Tobago	107	98	100	103	53	..	98	110
110	Bulgaria	110	..	97	106	76x	..	100	9
111	Sri Lanka	106	91	96	110	62	79	94	80
112	Colombia	109	100	101	120	66	52	81	200
113	Bosnia and Herzegovina	109	..	..	..	..	..	..	..
114	Poland	113	99x	98	105	75x	..	100x	11
115	Costa Rica	107	100	99	109	75	..	93	36
116	Chile	110	100	99	106	43x	..	98	35
117	Slovakia	112	..	..	..	74	..	..	..
118	Malaysia	106	85	101	107	48	..	87	59
119	Croatia	113	..	..	..	..	..	..	..
120	Hungary	114	99x	100	100	73	..	99x	15
121	Kuwait	105	91	102	100	35	44	99	6
122	Jamaica	107	110	103	112	66	..	82	120
123	Portugal	110	91	98	149	66x	..	90x	10
124	Cuba	105	99	99	113	70	61	90	39
125	United States	110	..	99	100	74	..	99	8
126	Czech Rep.	110	..	..	..	69	..	..	..
127	Belgium	110	..	102	101	79	..	100	3
128	Greece	107	91	101	98	..	..	97x	5
129	Spain	107	96	100	109	59	..	96	5
130	France	111	..	98	104	80	..	94x	9
131	Israel	104	94x	100	107	..	..	99	3
132	New Zealand	110	..	99	101	70x	..	99	13
133	Korea, Rep. of	112	96	102	101	79	..	89	26
134	Slovenia	115	..	..	..	..	..	..	..
135	Australia	107	..	100	102	76	..	99x	3
136	Italy	109	98	103	100	78x	..	..	4
137	Netherlands	108	..	103	96	76	..	100x	10
138	Norway	108	..	100	97	76	..	..	3
139	Canada	109	..	98	100	73	..	99	5
140	Austria	108	..	100	94	71	..	..	8
141	United Kingdom	108	..	101	104	72	..	100x	8
142	Switzerland	108	..	101	95	71	..	99x	5
143	Ireland	107	..	100	108	..	..	..	2
144	Germany	108	..	101	98	75	..	99	5
145	Denmark	108	..	100	102	78	..	100x	3
146	Japan	108	..	100	102	64	..	100	11
147	Hong Kong	108	89	99x	107x	81	..	100	6
148	Singapore	107	87	97	101	74	..	100	10
149	Finland	111	..	99	119	80x	..	100x	11
150	Sweden	108	..	100	101	78	..	100x	5

Countries listed in descending order of their 1994 under-five mortality rates (table 1).

Table 8: Basic indicators on less populous countries

| | | Under-5 mortality rate | | Infant mortality rate (under 1) | | Total population (thousands) | Annual no. of births (thousands) | Annual no. of under-5 deaths (thousands) | GNP per capita (US$) | Life expectancy at birth (years) | Total adult literacy rate | % of age group enrolled in primary school (gross) | % of children immunized against measles |
		1960	1994	1960	1994	1994	1994	1994	1993	1994	1985-90	1986-93	1991-94
1	Equatorial Guinea	316	177	188	114	389	17.0	3.0	420	48	73	149x	61
2	Djibouti	289	158	186	113	566	21.0	3.3	780	48	41	41	75
3	Comoros	248	126	165	86	630	30.0	3.8	560	56	54	79	59
4	Swaziland	233	107	157	74	832	32.0	3.4	1190	57	72	115	94
5	Marshall Islands	..	92	..	63	52	1.4x	0.1	a	..	91	95	86
6	Sao Tome/Principe	..	82	..	64	130	4.6	0.4	350	68	57x	..	57
7	Kiribati	..	78	..	58	77	2.2	0.2	710	57	93	91	77
8	Maldives	258	78	158	56	246	10.0	0.8	820	62	92	25	96
9	Cape Verde	164	73	110	54	381	14.0	1.0	920	64	63	116	83
10	Guyana	126	61	100	46	825	20.0	1.2	350	65	97	112	83
11	Vanuatu	225	59	141	45	165	6.0	0.4	1230	65	64	103	66
12	Tuvalu	..	56	..	40	9	..	..	650x	..	99	101	88
13	Samoa	210	55	134	44	169	6.0	0.3	950	67	98	100	94
14	St.Kitts/Nevis	..	41	..	33	41	0.9	0.0	4410	71	90	..	..
15	Belize	104	41	74	32	210	7.0	0.3	2450	73	70	90	90
16	Palau	..	35	..	25	17	0.3x	0.0	790x	..	98	103	92
17	Grenada	..	34	..	27	92	2.1	0.1	2380	71	91	88	87
18	Suriname	96	33	70	27	418	10.0	0.3	1180	70	92	127	69
19	Solomon Islands	185	32	120	26	366	14.0	0.5	740	70	62	90	64
20	Turks/Caicos Islands	..	31	..	25	14	0.2x	0.0	780x	..	98x	..	..
21	British Virgin Islands	..	29	..	25	18	0.2x	0.0	8500x	..	98x	..	100
22	Micronesia, Fed. States of	..	29	..	23	121	4.0	0.1	980x	71	81	100	..
23	Bahamas	68	28	51	23	272	5.0	0.1	11420	73	98	105	88
24	Cook Islands	..	28	..	26	19	0.4x	0.0	1550x	..	99	98	99
25	Fiji	97	27	71	22	771	18.0	0.5	2130	71	89	128	96
26	Tonga	..	24	..	20	98	2.7	0.1	1530	68	99	98	85
27	Qatar	239	24	145	19	540	11.0	0.3	15030	70	77	95	86
28	Antigua/Barbuda	..	23	..	19	65	1.0	0.0	6540	75	95	100	100
29	St. Vincent/Grenadines	..	23	..	19	111	2.2	0.1	2120	72	82	95	100
30	Saint Lucia	..	22	..	18	141	3.6	0.1	3380	73	82x	95	92
31	Dominica	..	21	..	17	71	1.5	0.0	2720	73	94x	..	99
32	Bahrain	203	20	130	17	549	15.0	0.3	8030	71	82	93	90
33	Seychelles	..	20	..	16	73	1.7	0.0	6280	72	88	102	99
34	Montserrat	..	14	..	12	11	0.2	0.0	3330x	75	97x	100	100
35	Malta	42	12	37	10	364	5.0	0.1	7970	76	86	110	90
36	Barbados	90	10	74	9	261	4.0	0.0	6230	76	97	106	97
37	Cyprus	36	10	30	9	734	13.0	0.1	10380	77	94	102	83
38	Brunei Darussalam	87	10	63	8	280	7.0	0.1	14144	74	85	113	92
39	Luxembourg	41	9	33	8	401	5.0	0.1	37320	76	..	90	80
40	Iceland	22	5	17	5	266	5.0	0.0	24950	78	..	100	98

a: Range US$696 to US$2785.

Measuring human development

An introduction to table 9

If development in the 1990s is to assume a more human face then there arises a corresponding need for a means of measuring human as well as economic progress. From UNICEF's point of view, in particular, there is a need for an agreed method of measuring the level of child well-being and its rate of change.

The under-five mortality rate (U5MR) is used in table 9 (next page) as the principal indicator of such progress.

The U5MR has several advantages. First, it measures an end result of the development process rather than an 'input' such as school enrolment level, per capita calorie availability, or the number of doctors per thousand population—all of which are means to an end.

Second, the U5MR is known to be the result of a wide variety of inputs: the nutritional health and the health knowledge of mothers; the level of immunization and ORT use; the availability of maternal and child health services (including prenatal care); income and food availability in the family; the availability of clean water and safe sanitation; and the overall safety of the child's environment.

Third, the U5MR is less susceptible than, say, per capita GNP to the fallacy of the average. This is because the natural scale does not allow the children of the rich to be one thousand times as likely to survive, even if the man-made scale does permit them to have one thousand times as much income. In other words, it is much more difficult for a wealthy minority to affect a nation's U5MR, and it therefore presents a more accurate, if far from perfect, picture of the health status of the majority of children (and of society as a whole).

For these reasons, the U5MR is chosen by UNICEF as its single most important indicator of the state of a nation's children. That is why the statistical annex lists the nations of the world not in ascending order of their per capita GNP but in descending order of their under-five mortality rates.

The speed of progress in reducing the U5MR can be measured by calculating its average annual reduction rate (AARR). Unlike the comparison of absolute changes, the AARR reflects the fact that the lower limits to U5MR are approached only with increasing difficulty. As lower levels of under-five mortality are reached, for example, the same absolute reduction obviously represents a greater percentage of reduction. The AARR therefore shows a higher rate of progress for, say, a 10-point reduction if that reduction happens at a lower level of under-five mortality. (A fall in U5MR of 10 points from 100 to 90 represents a reduction of 10 per cent, whereas the same 10-point fall from 20 to 10 represents a reduction of 50 per cent).

When used in conjunction with GNP growth rates, the U5MR and its reduction rate can therefore give a picture of the progress being made by any country or region, and over any period of time, towards the satisfaction of some of the most essential of human needs.

As table 9 shows, there is no fixed relationship between the annual reduction rate of the U5MR and the annual rate of growth in per capita GNP. Such comparisons help to throw the emphasis on to the policies, priorities, and other factors which determine the ratio between economic and social progress.

Finally, the table gives the total fertility rate for each country and its average annual rate of reduction. It will be seen that many of the nations which have achieved significant reductions in their U5MR have also achieved significant reductions in fertility.

Table 9: The rate of progress

		Under-5 mortality rate			average annual rate of reduction (%)		required*	GNP per capita average annual growth rate (%)		Total fertility rate			average annual rate of reduction (%)	
		1960	1980	1994	1960-80	1980-94	1994-2000	1965-80	1980-93	1960	1980	1994	1960-80	1980-94
1	Niger	320	320	320	0.0	0.0	25.3	-2.5	-4.1	7.3	8.1	7.3	-0.5	0.7
2	Angola	345	261	292	1.4	-0.8	23.8	..	-0.9x	6.4	6.9	7.0	-0.4	-0.1
3	Sierra Leone	385	301	284	1.2	0.4	23.3	0.7	-1.5	6.2	6.5	6.4	-0.2	0.1
4	Mozambique	331	269	277	1.0	-0.2	22.9	..	-1.5	6.3	6.5	6.4	-0.2	0.1
5	Afghanistan	360	280	257	1.3	0.6	21.7	0.6	..	6.9	7.1	6.7	-0.1	0.4
6	Guinea-Bissau	336	290	231	0.7	1.6	19.9	-2.7	2.8	5.1	5.7	5.7	-0.6	0.0
7	Guinea	337	276	223	1.0	1.5	19.3	1.3	1.3x	7.0	7.0	6.9	0.0	0.1
8	Malawi	365	290	221	1.1	1.9	19.2	3.2	-1.2	6.9	7.6	7.0	-0.5	0.6
9	Liberia	288	235	217	1.0	0.6	18.9	0.5	5.2x	6.6	6.8	6.7	-0.1	0.1
10	Mali	400	310	214	1.3	2.6	18.6	2.1x	-1.0	7.1	7.1	7.0	0.0	0.1
11	Gambia	375	278	213	1.5	1.9	18.5	..	-0.2	6.4	6.5	5.5	-0.1	1.2
12	Somalia	294	246	211	0.9	1.1	18.4	-0.1	-2.3x	7.0	7.0	6.9	0.0	0.1
13	Zambia	220	160	203	1.6	-1.7	17.7	-1.2	-3.1	6.6	7.1	5.8	-0.4	1.4
14	Chad	325	254	202	1.2	1.6	17.7	-1.9	3.2	6.0	5.9	5.8	0.1	0.1
15	Eritrea	294	260	200	0.6	1.9	17.5	..	..	6.6	6.1	5.7	0.4	0.5
16	Ethiopia	294	260	200	0.6	1.9	17.5	0.4	-1.8x	6.9	6.9	6.9	0.0	0.0
17	Mauritania	321	249	199	1.3	1.6	17.4	-0.1	-0.8	6.5	6.3	5.3	0.2	1.2
18	Bhutan	324	249	193	1.3	1.8	16.9	..	4.5x	6.0	5.9	5.7	0.1	0.2
19	Nigeria	204	196	191	0.2	0.2	16.7	4.2	-0.1	6.5	6.5	6.3	0.0	0.2
20	Zaire	286	204	186	1.7	0.6	16.3	-1.3	-0.8x	6.0	6.6	6.6	-0.5	0.0
21	Uganda	218	181	185	0.9	-0.2	16.2	-2.2	1.9x	6.9	7.0	7.1	-0.1	-0.1
22	Cambodia	217	330	177	-2.1	4.4	15.5	..	..	6.3	4.6	5.1	1.6	-0.7
23	Burundi	255	193	176	1.4	0.7	15.4	2.4	0.9	6.8	6.8	6.6	0.0	0.1
24	Central African Rep.	294	202	175	1.9	1.0	15.3	0.8	-1.6	5.6	5.8	5.6	-0.2	0.3
25	Burkina Faso	318	246	169	1.3	2.7	14.7	1.7	0.8	6.4	6.5	6.4	-0.1	0.1
26	Madagascar	364	216	164	2.6	2.0	14.2	-0.4	-2.6	6.6	6.6	6.0	0.0	0.7
27	Tanzania, U. Rep. of	249	202	159	1.0	1.7	13.7	0.8	0.1	6.8	6.8	5.8	0.0	1.1
28	Lesotho	204	173	156	0.8	0.7	13.4	6.8	-0.5	5.8	5.7	5.1	0.1	0.8
29	Gabon	287	194	151	2.0	1.8	12.8	5.6	-1.6	4.1	4.4	5.4	-0.4	-1.5
30	Côte d'Ivoire	300	170	150	2.8	0.9	12.7	2.8	-4.6	7.2	7.4	7.3	-0.1	0.1
31	Benin	310	176	142	2.8	1.6	11.8	-0.3	-0.4	6.9	7.1	7.0	-0.1	0.1
32	Rwanda	191	222	139	-0.8	3.3	11.4	1.6	-1.2	7.5	8.3	6.4	-0.5	1.9
33	Lao Peo. Dem. Rep.	233	190	138	1.0	2.3	11.3	..	2.1x	6.2	6.7	6.5	-0.4	0.2
34	Pakistan	221	151	137	1.9	0.7	11.2	1.8	3.1	6.9	7.0	6.0	-0.1	1.1
35	Togo	264	175	132	2.0	2.0	10.6	1.7	-2.1	6.6	6.6	6.4	0.0	0.2
36	Ghana	213	155	131	1.6	1.2	10.4	-0.8	0.1	6.9	6.5	5.8	0.3	0.8
37	Haiti	260	195	127	1.4	3.1	9.9	0.9	-3.4x	6.3	5.3	4.7	0.9	0.9
38	Sudan	292	200	122	1.9	3.6	9.2	0.8	-0.2x	6.7	6.5	5.6	0.2	1.1
39	India	236	177	119	1.4	2.8	8.8	1.5	3.0	5.9	4.7	3.7	1.1	1.7
40	Nepal	290	180	118	2.4	3.0	8.7	..	2.0	5.7	6.4	5.3	-0.6	1.3
41	Bangladesh	247	211	117	0.8	4.2	8.6	-0.3	2.1	6.7	6.4	4.2	0.2	3.0
42	Senegal	303	221	115	1.6	4.6	8.3	-0.5	0.0	7.0	6.9	5.9	0.1	1.1
43	Yemen	340	210	112	2.4	4.5	7.8	..	..	7.6	7.6	7.5	0.0	0.1
44	Indonesia	216	128	111	2.6	1.0	7.7	5.2	4.2	5.5	4.4	2.8	1.1	3.2
45	Bolivia	252	170	110	2.0	3.1	7.6	1.7	-0.7	6.7	5.6	4.7	0.9	1.3
46	Cameroon	264	173	109	2.1	3.3	7.4	2.4	-2.2	5.8	6.4	5.6	-0.5	1.0
47	Congo	220	125	109	2.8	1.0	7.4	2.7	-0.3	5.9	6.3	6.2	-0.3	0.1
48	Myanmar	237	146	109	2.4	2.1	7.4	1.6	..	6.0	5.1	4.1	0.8	1.6
49	Libyan Arab Jamahiriya	269	150	95	2.9	3.2	5.1	0.0	-9.2x	7.1	7.3	6.2	-0.1	1.2
50	Papua New Guinea	248	95	95	4.8	0.0	6.8	..	0.6	6.3	5.7	4.9	0.5	1.1
51	Kenya	202	112	90	2.9	1.6	6.8	3.1	0.3	8.0	7.8	6.1	0.1	1.8
52	Turkmenistan	..	..	87	..	..	..	..	-1.6x	6.4	5.1	3.9	1.1	1.9
53	Tajikistan	..	..	81	..	..	..	..	-3.6	6.3	5.7	4.8	0.5	1.2
54	Zimbabwe	181	125	81	1.8	3.1	5.0	1.7	-0.3	7.5	6.4	4.9	0.8	1.9
55	Namibia	206	114	78	3.0	2.7	5.7	..	0.7	6.0	5.9	5.1	0.1	1.0
56	Mongolia	185	112	76	2.5	2.7	5.0	..	0.2	6.0	5.4	3.5	0.5	3.1
57	Iraq	171	83	71	3.6	1.1	13.4	7.2	6.5	5.6	0.5	1.1		
58	Guatemala	205	136	70	2.0	4.7	3.6	3.0	-1.2	6.9	6.3	5.2	0.5	1.4
59	South Africa	126	91	68	1.6	2.1	5.6	3.2	-0.2	6.5	4.9	4.0	1.4	1.4
60	Nicaragua	209	143	68	1.9	5.3	2.8	-0.7	-5.7	7.4	6.2	4.9	0.9	1.7
61	Algeria	243	145	65	2.6	5.7	3.4	4.2	-0.8	7.3	6.8	3.7	0.4	4.3
62	Uzbekistan	..	..	64	..	..	..	..	-0.2	6.3	4.9	3.8	1.3	1.8
63	Brazil	181	93	61	3.3	3.0	4.6	6.3	0.3	6.2	3.9	2.8	2.3	2.4
64	Peru	236	130	58	3.0	5.8	2.7	0.8	-2.7	6.9	5.0	3.3	1.6	3.0
65	Philippines	102	70	57	1.9	1.4	5.4	3.2	-0.6	6.9	4.9	3.8	1.7	1.8
66	Ecuador	180	101	57	2.9	4.1	5.0	5.4	0.0	6.7	5.1	3.4	1.4	2.9
67	El Salvador	210	120	56	2.8	5.4	3.1	1.5	0.2	6.8	5.4	3.9	1.2	2.3
68	Morocco	215	145	56	2.0	6.7	2.6	2.7	1.2	7.2	5.5	3.6	1.3	3.0
69	Kyrgyzstan	..	..	56	..	..	..	..	0.1	5.1	4.1	3.6	1.1	0.9
70	Turkey	217	141	55	2.2	6.7	0.5	3.6	2.4	6.3	4.3	3.3	1.9	1.9
71	Botswana	170	94	54	3.0	3.9	4.6	9.9	6.2	6.8	6.1	4.7	0.5	1.9
72	Honduras	203	100	54	3.6	4.4	4.3	1.1	-0.3	7.5	6.3	4.7	0.9	2.1
73	Egypt	258	180	52	1.8	8.9	-0.4	2.8	2.8	7.0	5.2	3.7	1.5	2.4
74	Azerbaijan	..	..	51	..	..	..	..	-3.5	5.5	3.3	2.4	2.6	2.3
75	Iran, Islamic Rep. of	233	126	51	3.1	6.5	2.1	2.9	-0.7x	7.2	6.7	4.9	0.4	2.2

96

		Under-5 mortality rate			average annual rate of reduction (%)			GNP per capita average annual growth rate (%)		Total fertility rate			average annual rate of reduction (%)	
		1960	1980	1994	1960-80	1980-94	required* 1994-2000	1965-80	1980-93	1960	1980	1994	1960-80	1980-94
76	Kazakhstan	..	..	48	..	..	..		-1.6	4.5	3.0	2.5	2.0	1.3
77	Viet Nam	219	105	46	3.7	5.9	3.9	..	4.8x	6.1	5.1	3.8	0.9	2.1
78	Dominican Rep.	152	94	45	2.4	5.2	3.2	3.8	0.7	7.4	4.3	3.0	2.7	2.6
79	China	209	65	43	5.9	2.9	6.7	4.1	8.2	5.5	2.9	2.0	3.2	2.7
80	Albania	151	57	41	4.9	2.4	6.8	..	-3.2	5.9	3.8	2.8	2.2	2.2
81	Lebanon	85	40	40	3.8	0.0	6.7	..	..	6.3	4.0	3.0	2.3	2.1
82	Syrian Arab Rep.	201	73	38	5.1	4.7	4.2	5.1	-2.1x	7.3	7.4	5.7	-0.1	1.9
83	Moldova	..	..	36	..	..	..		-2.0	3.3	2.5	2.1	1.4	1.2
84	Saudi Arabia	292	90	36	5.9	6.6	2.9	4.0x	-3.6	7.2	7.3	6.2	-0.1	1.2
85	Paraguay	90	61	34	1.9	4.2	5.3	4.1	-0.7	6.8	4.8	4.2	1.7	1.0
86	Tunisia	244	102	34	4.4	7.8	1.7	4.7	1.2	7.1	5.3	3.0	1.5	4.1
87	Thailand	146	61	32	4.4	4.5	4.8	4.4	6.4	6.4	3.6	2.1	2.9	3.9
88	Armenia	..	..	32	..	..	..		-4.2	4.5	2.4	2.5	3.1	-0.3
89	TFYR Macedonia	177	69	32	4.7	5.5	2.6	..	..	4.2	2.6	2.0	2.4	1.9
90	Mexico	148	87	32	2.7	7.2	3.4	3.6	-0.5	6.8	4.7	3.1	1.8	3.0
91	Russian Federation	..	..	31	..	..	..		-1.0	2.6	2.0	1.5	1.3	2.1
92	Korea, Dem. Peo. Rep.	120	43	31	5.1	2.5	4.6	..	..	5.8	3.1	2.3	3.1	2.1
93	Romania	82	36	29	4.1	1.5	4.6	..	-2.4	2.3	2.4	1.5	-0.2	3.4
94	Georgia	..	..	27	..	..	..		-6.6	2.9	2.3	2.1	1.2	0.6
95	Argentina	68	41	27	2.5	3.0	6.7	1.7	-0.5	3.1	3.3	2.7	-0.3	1.4
96	Oman	300	95	27	5.7	9.0	2.3	9.0	3.4	7.2	7.2	7.0	0.0	0.2
97	Latvia	..	..	26	..	..	..	..	-0.6	1.9	2.0	1.6	-0.3	1.6
98	Ukraine	..	..	25	..	..	..	..	0.2	2.2	2.0	1.6	0.5	1.6
99	Jordan	149	66	25	4.1	6.9	1.2	5.8x	-5.9x	7.7	7.1	5.4	0.4	2.0
100	Venezuela	70	42	24	2.6	4.0	5.2	2.3	-0.7	6.6	4.2	3.2	2.3	1.9
101	Estonia	..	..	23	..	..	..	..	-2.2	2.0	2.1	1.6	-0.2	1.9
102	Yugoslavia	120	44	23	5.0	4.6	2.3	..	..	2.7	2.3	2.0	0.8	1.0
103	Mauritius	84	42	23	3.4	4.4	4.7	3.7	5.5	5.8	2.8	2.3	3.6	1.4
104	Belarus	..	..	21	..	..	..		2.4	2.7	2.1	1.7	1.3	1.5
105	Uruguay	47	42	21	0.6	4.9	4.9	2.5	-0.1	2.9	2.7	2.3	0.4	1.1
106	United Arab Emirates	240	64	20	6.6	8.2	3.9	..	-4.4	6.9	5.4	4.1	1.2	2.0
107	Lithuania	..	..	20	..	..	..	..	-2.8	2.5	2.1	1.8	0.9	1.1
108	Panama	104	31	20	6.0	3.1	6.1	2.8	-0.7	5.9	3.8	2.8	2.2	2.2
109	Trinidad and Tobago	73	40	20	3.0	5.0	3.4	3.1	-2.8	5.1	3.3	2.4	2.2	2.3
110	Bulgaria	70	25	19	5.1	1.8	8.0	..	0.5	2.2	2.1	1.5	0.2	2.4
111	Sri Lanka	130	52	19	4.6	7.2	3.6	2.8	2.7	5.3	3.5	2.4	2.1	2.7
112	Colombia	132	59	19	4.1	8.1	4.9	3.7	1.5	6.8	3.8	2.6	2.9	2.7
113	Bosnia and Herzegovina	155	38	17	7.0	5.7	4.1	..	..	4.0	2.1	1.6	3.2	1.9
114	Poland	70	24	16	5.3	2.9	5.0	..	0.4	3.0	2.3	1.9	1.3	1.4
115	Costa Rica	112	29	16	6.8	4.2	6.7	3.3	1.1	7.0	3.7	3.1	3.2	1.3
116	Chile	138	35	15	6.9	5.9	2.1	0.0	3.6	5.3	2.8	2.5	3.2	0.8
117	Slovakia	..	..	15	..	..	..	..	..	3.1	2.4	1.9	1.3	1.7
118	Malaysia	105	42	15	4.6	7.4	1.4	4.7	3.5	6.8	4.2	3.5	2.4	1.3
119	Croatia	98	23	14	7.2	3.3	6.8	..	..	2.3	2.0	1.7	0.7	1.2
120	Hungary	57	26	14	3.9	4.5	3.9	5.1	1.2	2.0	2.0	1.7	0.0	1.2
121	Kuwait	128	35	14	6.6	6.6	3.7	0.6x	-4.3	7.3	5.4	3.0	1.5	4.2
122	Jamaica	76	39	13	3.4	8.0	2.9	-0.1	-0.3	5.4	3.8	2.3	1.8	3.6
123	Portugal	112	31	11	6.4	7.4	0.5	4.6	3.3	3.1	2.2	1.6	1.7	2.3
124	Cuba	50	26	10	3.3	6.5	3.0	..	..	4.2	2.0	1.8	3.7	0.8
125	United States	30	15	10	3.3	3.0	5.2	1.8	1.7	3.5	1.8	2.1	3.3	-1.1
126	Czech Rep.	..	..	10	..	..	..	..	-2.0x	2.3	2.2	1.8	0.2	1.4
127	Belgium	35	15	10	4.3	3.2	6.8	3.6	1.9	2.6	1.6	1.7	2.4	-0.4
128	Greece	64	23	10	5.2	6.3	4.2	4.8	0.9	2.2	2.1	1.4	0.2	2.9
129	Spain	57	16	9	6.2	4.0	6.5	4.1	2.7	2.8	2.2	1.2	1.2	4.3
130	France	34	13	9	4.9	2.5	6.3	3.7	1.6	2.8	1.9	1.7	1.9	0.8
131	Israel	39	19	9	3.6	5.7	1.8	3.7	2.0	3.9	3.3	2.8	0.8	1.2
132	New Zealand	26	16	9	2.5	4.3	0.6	1.7	0.7	3.9	2.1	2.1	3.1	0.0
133	Korea, Rep. of	124	18	9	9.8	5.2	3.5	7.3	8.2	5.7	2.6	1.8	3.9	2.6
134	Slovenia	45	18	8	4.6	5.6	3.4	..	..	2.4	2.1	1.5	0.7	2.4
135	Australia	24	13	8	3.0	3.8	3.8	2.2	1.6	3.3	2.0	1.9	2.5	0.4
136	Italy	50	17	8	5.3	5.6	3.0	3.2	2.1	2.5	1.7	1.3	1.9	1.9
137	Netherlands	22	11	8	3.4	2.6	4.8	2.7	1.7	3.1	1.5	1.6	3.6	-0.5
138	Norway	23	11	8	3.8	2.4	2.9	3.6	2.2	2.9	1.8	2.0	2.4	-0.8
139	Canada	33	13	8	4.8	3.8	4.6	3.3	1.4	3.8	1.7	1.9	4.0	-0.8
140	Austria	43	17	7	4.6	6.0	2.7	4.0	2.0	2.7	1.6	1.6	2.6	0.0
141	United Kingdom	27	14	7	3.1	4.7	3.2	2.0	2.3	2.7	1.8	1.8	2.0	0.0
142	Switzerland	27	11	7	4.5	2.9	3.0	1.5	1.1	2.4	1.5	1.6	2.4	-0.5
143	Ireland	36	14	7	4.6	4.9	3.0	2.8	3.6	3.8	3.2	2.1	0.9	3.0
144	Germany	40	16	7	4.7	5.9	2.6	3.0x	2.1	2.4	1.5	1.3	2.4	1.0
145	Denmark	25	10	7	4.4	3.0	2.1	2.2	2.0	2.6	1.6	1.7	2.4	-0.4
146	Japan	40	11	6	6.6	3.8	6.9	5.1	3.4	2.0	1.8	1.5	0.5	1.3
147	Hong Kong	52	13	6	6.9	5.5	3.4	6.2	5.4	5.0	2.1	1.2	4.3	4.0
148	Singapore	40	13	6	5.6	6.1	0.6	8.3	6.1	5.5	1.8	1.7	5.6	0.4
149	Finland	28	9	5	5.9	3.8	2.1	3.6	1.5	2.7	1.7	1.9	2.3	-0.8
150	Sweden	20	9	5	4.1	4.2	1.4	2.0	1.3	2.3	1.6	2.1	1.8	-1.9

* The average annual reduction rate required to achieve an under-five mortality rate in all countries of 70 per 1000 live births or of two thirds the 1990 rate, whichever is the less.
Countries listed in descending order of their 1994 under-five mortality rates.

Table 10: Regional summaries

	Sub-Saharan Africa	Middle East and North Africa	South Asia	East Asia and Pacific	Latin America and Caribbean	Countries in transition	Industrialized countries	Developing countries	Least developed countries
Table 1: Basic indicators									
Under-5 mortality rate 1960	256	239	238	200	159	..	37	216	282
Under-5 mortality rate 1994	177	62	124	56	47	36	9	101	170
Infant mortality rate 1960	153	156	146	133	106	..	31	138	171
Infant mortality rate 1994	107	48	84	42	38	30	7	68	108
Total population (millions)	548	363	1233	1764	466	414	823	4373	557
Annual no. of births (thousands)	24332	11676	37911	35690	11856	5647	10526	121465	23520
Annual no. of under-5 deaths (thousands)	4306	728	4700	2005	557	202	90	12296	3998
GNP per capita (US$)	519	2129	309	871	2883	2000	23195	987	238
Life expectancy at birth (years)	51	64	59	66	68	70	77	61	51
Total adult literacy rate (%)	52	58	46	80	85	98	95	67	45
% enrolled in primary school	70	96	91	116	106	..	103	99	66
% share of household income, lowest 40%	..	..	21	18	9	..	18	..	..
% share of household income, highest 20%	..	..	41	44	62	..	41	..	..
Table 2: Nutrition									
% with low birth weight	16	10	33	11	11	..	6	19	24
% of children who are exclusively breastfed, 0-3 months	26	..	47	..	19	..	..	..	44
% of children who are breastfed with food, 6-9 months	64	..	..	..	..	..	..	..	..
% of children who are still breastfeeding, 20-23 months	43	..	..	..	20	..	..	..	..
% of children suffering from underweight, moderate & severe	31	12	64	23	11	..	..	35	41
% of children suffering from underweight, severe	9	..	24	..	2	..	..	12	13
% of children suffering from wasting, moderate & severe	7	5	13	4	3	..	..	6	10
% of children suffering from stunting, moderate & severe	41	24	62	33	21	..	..	42	50
Total goitre rate (%)	16	22	13	13	15	15	..	15	19
Calorie supply as % of requirements	93	124	99	112	114	..	134	107	91
% share of household consumption, all foods	38	39	51	45	34	..	14	41	..
% share of household consumption, cereals	15	10	19	..	8	..	2	..	..
Table 3: Health									
% with access to safe water, total	45	76	80	66	80	..	..	70	52
% with access to safe water, urban	63	93	87	92	87	..	..	87	65
% with access to safe water, rural	34	58	78	56	51	..	..	60	48
% with access to adequate sanitation, total	37	62	30	34	68	..	..	39	32
% with access to adequate sanitation, urban	56	87	69	75	71	..	..	72	62
% with access to adequate sanitation, rural	29	35	17	17	36	..	..	20	25
% with access to health services, total	57	85	77	89	73	..	..	80	51
% with access to health services, urban	79	97	..	98	81	..	..	94	81
% with access to health services, rural	50	72	..	..	51	..	..	76	43
% of 1-year-olds immunized against TB	64	89	91	94	93	87	85	87	71
% of 1-year-olds immunized against DPT	51	83	86	91	82	78	88	80	60
% of 1-year-olds immunized against polio	48	84	85	92	80	82	84	80	59
% of 1-year-olds immunized against measles	51	84	82	89	83	88	81	78	61
% of pregnant women immunized against tetanus	35	49	71	29	48	..	..	47	43
ORT use rate (%)	50	58	46	76	64	..	..	59	56
Table 4: Education									
Adult literacy rate 1970, male (%)	40	49	46	76	76	..	98	55	40
Adult literacy rate 1970, female (%)	18	20	17	55	69	..	96	32	14
Adult literacy rate 1990, male (%)	63	70	59	88	86	99	..	76	56
Adult literacy rate 1990, female (%)	42	46	32	72	83	97	..	57	34
No. of radio sets per 1000 population	142	240	79	195	344	..	1253	176	95
No. of television sets per 1000 population	23	112	31	44	163	..	593	56	10
Primary school enrolment ratio (%) 1960 (gross), male	47	72	77	120	75	..	109	93	48
Primary school enrolment ratio (%) 1960 (gross), female	24	40	39	85	71	..	109	62	23
Primary school enrolment ratio (%) 1986-93 (gross), male	76	103	102	119	105	..	103	105	73
Primary school enrolment ratio (%) 1986-93 (gross), female	63	89	80	112	103	..	102	92	58
Primary school enrolment ratio (%) 1986-93 (net), male	55	90	..	99	82	..	98	87	57
Primary school enrolment ratio (%) 1986-93 (net), female	47	81	..	94	82	..	98	80	46
% reaching grade 5, primary school	66	91	59	87	74	..	98	74	54
Secondary school enrolment ratio, male (%)	24	61	52	56	46	..	95	50	21
Secondary school enrolment ratio, female (%)	21	46	32	48	49	..	96	40	12

	Sub-Saharan Africa	Middle East and North Africa	South Asia	East Asia and Pacific	Latin America and Caribbean	Countries in transition	Industrialized countries	Developing countries	Least developed countries
Table 5: Demographic indicators									
Population under 16 (millions)	262	154	482	540	170	105	169	1607	256
Population under 5 (millions)	100	53	166	173	56	29	53	549	96
Population annual growth rate 1965-80 (%)	2.7	2.8	2.3	2.2	2.5	0.9	0.8	2.3	2.6
Population annual growth rate 1980-94 (%)	2.9	2.9	2.2	1.6	2.0	0.6	0.6	2.1	2.6
Crude death rate 1960	24	21	21	19	13	9	10	20	25
Crude death rate 1994	15	8	10	7	7	11	9	9	15
Crude birth rate 1960	49	47	44	39	42	23	20	42	48
Crude birth rate 1994	45	33	31	21	26	15	13	29	43
Life expectancy 1960 (years)	41	48	44	49	56	67	70	47	40
Life expectancy 1994 (years)	51	64	59	66	68	70	77	61	51
Total fertility rate	6.2	4.4	4.0	2.3	3.0	1.9	1.7	3.5	5.7
% of population urbanized	31	55	26	32	74	65	77	37	22
Urban population annual growth rate 1965-80 (%)	5.2	4.6	3.8	3.3	3.8	2.1	1.3	3.8	5.4
Urban population annual growth rate 1980-94 (%)	5.0	4.4	3.5	4.2	2.9	1.2	0.8	3.8	4.9
Table 6: Economic indicators									
GNP per capita (US$)	519	2129	309	871	2883	2000	23195	987	238
GNP per capita annual growth rate 1965-80 (%)	2.7	3.2	1.5	4.9	4.0	. .	2.9	3.7	0.0
GNP per capita annual growth rate 1980-93 (%)	-0.3	0.6	2.9	6.8	-0.1	-0.6	2.2	2.9	0.7
Annual rate of inflation (%)	15	28	9	8	247	36	5	93	16
% below absolute poverty level, urban	. .	. .	33	. .	18	. .	. .	27	55
% below absolute poverty level, rural	62	. .	39	16	48	. .	. .	31	70
% of government expenditure to health	4	5	2	2	5	. .	14	4	5
% of government expenditure to education	12	17	3	10	10	. .	4	10	13
% of government expenditure to defence	9	18	16	16	5	. .	12	13	14
ODA inflow (US$ millions)	15865	5743	5153	8947	4548	446	1316	40256	14341
ODA inflow as % of recipient GNP	10	1	2	1	0	. .	. .	1	15
Debt service, % of goods & services exports 1970	5	. .	17	6	13	. .	. .	11	5
Debt service, % of goods & services exports 1993	12	21	21	9	18	7	. .	14	10
Table 7: Women									
Life expectancy, females as % of males	107	104	101	105	108	114	109	104	104
Adult literacy, females as % of males	68	66	54	81	97	98	. .	75	60
Enrolment, females as % of males, primary school	83	86	78	94	98	. .	100	88	80
Enrolment, females as % of males, secondary school	87	76	61	85	108	. .	102	79	60
Contraceptive prevalence (%)	13	44	40	74	59	. .	72	55	17
Pregnant women immunized against tetanus (%)	35	49	71	29	48	. .	. .	47	43
% of births attended by trained health personnel	38	57	30	82	81	. .	99	56	29
Maternal mortality rate	597	200	482	165	178	. .	7	346	603
Table 9: The rate of progress									
Under-5 mortality rate 1960	256	239	237	200	158	. .	37	216	281
Under-5 mortality rate 1980	204	142	179	80	87	. .	14	138	222
Under-5 mortality rate 1994	177	62	124	56	47	36	9	101	170
Under-5 mortality annual reduction rate 1960-80 (%)	1.1	2.6	1.4	4.6	3.0	. .	4.6	2.2	1.2
Under-5 mortality annual reduction rate 1980-94 (%)	1.0	5.9	2.6	2.5	4.4	. .	3.8	2.2	1.9
Under-5 mortality annual reduction rate required 1994-2000 (%)	15.9	4.1	9.6	6.9	4.5	. .	4.8	10.2	14.8
GNP per capita annual growth rate 1965-80 (%)	2.7	3.2	1.5	4.9	4.0	. .	2.9	3.7	0.0
GNP per capita annual growth rate 1980-93 (%)	-0.3	0.6	2.9	6.8	-0.1	-0.6	2.2	2.9	0.7
Total fertility rate 1960	6.6	7.0	6.1	5.6	6.0	2.8	2.8	6.0	6.6
Total fertility rate 1980	6.6	5.9	5.1	3.3	4.1	2.3	1.8	4.4	6.5
Total fertility rate 1994	6.2	4.4	4.0	2.3	3.0	1.9	1.7	3.5	5.7
Total fertility annual reduction rate 1960-80 (%)	0.0	0.9	0.8	2.7	1.9	0.9	2.3	1.5	0.0
Total fertility annual reduction rate 1980-94 (%)	0.5	2.0	1.7	2.5	2.2	1.5	0.2	1.8	1.0

Figures in this table are totals or weighted averages.

Country groupings for table 10

Sub-Saharan Africa

Angola	Ethiopia	Mali	South Africa
Benin	Gabon	Mauritania	Tanzania, U. Rep. of
Botswana	Gambia	Mauritius	Togo
Burkina Faso	Ghana	Mozambique	Uganda
Burundi	Guinea	Namibia	Zaire
Cameroon	Guinea-Bissau	Niger	Zambia
Central African Rep.	Kenya	Nigeria	Zimbabwe
Chad	Lesotho	Rwanda	
Congo	Liberia	Senegal	
Côte d'Ivoire	Madagascar	Sierra Leone	
Eritrea	Malawi	Somalia	

Middle East and North Africa

Algeria	Kuwait	Saudi Arabia	United Arab Emirates
Egypt	Lebanon	Sudan	Yemen
Iran, Islamic Rep. of	Libyan Arab Jamahiriya	Syrian Arab Rep.	
Iraq	Morocco	Tunisia	
Jordan	Oman	Turkey	

South Asia

Afghanistan	India	Sri Lanka
Bangladesh	Nepal	
Bhutan	Pakistan	

East Asia and Pacific

Cambodia	Korea, Dem. Peo. Rep.	Mongolia	Singapore
China	Korea, Rep. of	Myanmar	Thailand
Hong Kong	Lao Peo. Dem. Rep.	Papua New Guinea	Viet Nam
Indonesia	Malaysia	Philippines	

Latin America and Caribbean

Argentina	Cuba	Honduras	Peru
Bolivia	Dominican Rep.	Jamaica	Trinidad and Tobago
Brazil	Ecuador	Mexico	Uruguay
Chile	El Salvador	Nicaragua	Venezuela
Colombia	Guatemala	Panama	
Costa Rica	Haiti	Paraguay	

Countries in transition

Albania	Czech Republic	Lithuania	Tajikistan
Armenia	Estonia	Moldova	TFYR Macedonia
Azerbaijan	Georgia	Poland	Turkmenistan
Belarus	Hungary	Romania	Ukraine
Bosnia and Herzegovina	Kazakhstan	Russian Federation	Uzbekistan
Bulgaria	Kyrgyzstan	Slovakia	Yugoslavia
Croatia	Latvia	Slovenia	

Industrialized countries	Australia	France	Japan	Sweden
	Austria	Germany	Netherlands	Switzerland
	Belgium	Greece	New Zealand	United Kingdom
	Canada	Ireland	Norway	United States
	Denmark	Israel	Portugal	
	Finland	Italy	Spain	

Developing countries	Afghanistan	El Salvador	Libyan Arab Jamahiriya	Senegal
	Algeria	Eritrea	Madagascar	Sierra Leone
	Angola	Ethiopia	Malawi	Singapore
	Argentina	Gabon	Malaysia	Somalia
	Bangladesh	Gambia	Mali	South Africa
	Benin	Ghana	Mauritania	Sri Lanka
	Bhutan	Guatemala	Mauritius	Sudan
	Bolivia	Guinea	Mexico	Syrian Arab Rep.
	Botswana	Guinea-Bissau	Mongolia	Tanzania, U. Rep. of
	Brazil	Haiti	Morocco	Thailand
	Burkina Faso	Honduras	Mozambique	Togo
	Burundi	Hong Kong	Myanmar	Trinidad and Tobago
	Cambodia	India	Namibia	Tunisia
	Cameroon	Indonesia	Nepal	Turkey
	Central African Rep.	Iran, Islamic Rep. of	Nicaragua	Uganda
	Chad	Iraq	Niger	United Arab Emirates
	Chile	Jamaica	Nigeria	Uruguay
	China	Jordan	Oman	Venezuela
	Colombia	Kenya	Pakistan	Viet Nam
	Congo	Korea, Dem. Peo. Rep.	Panama	Yemen
	Costa Rica	Korea, Rep. of	Papua New Guinea	Zaire
	Côte d'Ivoire	Kuwait	Paraguay	Zambia
	Cuba	Lao Peo. Dem. Rep.	Peru	Zimbabwe
	Dominican Rep.	Lebanon	Philippines	
	Ecuador	Lesotho	Rwanda	
	Egypt	Liberia	Saudi Arabia	

Least developed countries	Afghanistan	Chad	Madagascar	Sierra Leone
	Bangladesh	Ethiopia	Malawi	Somalia
	Benin	Gambia	Mali	Sudan
	Bhutan	Guinea	Mauritania	Tanzania, U. Rep. of
	Botswana	Guinea-Bissau	Mozambique	Togo
	Burkina Faso	Haiti	Myanmar	Uganda
	Burundi	Lao Peo. Dem. Rep.	Nepal	Yemen
	Cambodia	Lesotho	Niger	Zaire
	Central African Rep.	Liberia	Rwanda	Zambia

Definitions

Under-five mortality rate
Probability of dying between birth and exactly five years of age expressed per 1,000 live births.

Infant mortality rate
Probability of dying between birth and exactly one year of age expressed per 1,000 live births.

GNP
Gross national product, expressed in current United States dollars. GNP per capita growth rates are average annual growth rates that have been computed by fitting trend lines to the logarithmic values of GNP per capita at constant market prices for each year of the time period.

Life expectancy at birth
The number of years newborn children would live if subject to the mortality risks prevailing for the cross-section of population at the time of their birth.

Adult literacy rate
Percentage of persons aged 15 and over who can read and write.

Primary and secondary enrolment ratios
The gross enrolment ratio is the total number of children enrolled in a schooling level— whether or not they belong in the relevant age group for that level—expressed as a percentage of the total number of children in the relevant age group for that level. The net enrolment ratio is the total number of children enrolled in a schooling level who belong in the relevant age group, expressed as a percentage of the total number in that age group.

Income share
Percentage of income received by the 20 per cent of households with the highest income and by the 40 per cent of households with the lowest income.

Low birth weight
Less than 2,500 grams.

Underweight
Moderate and severe—below minus two standard deviations from median weight for age of reference population;
severe—below minus three standard deviations from median weight for age of reference population.

Wasting
Moderate and severe—below minus two standard deviations from median weight for height of reference population.

Stunting
Moderate and severe—below minus two standard deviations from median height for age of reference population.

Total goitre rate
Percentage of children aged 6-11 with palpable or visible goitre. This is an indicator of iodine deficiency, which causes brain damage and mental retardation.

Access to health services
Percentage of the population that can reach appropriate local health services by the local means of transport in no more than one hour.

DPT
Diphtheria, pertussis (whooping cough) and tetanus.

ORT use
Percentage of all cases of diarrhoea in children under five years of age treated with oral rehydration salts or an appropriate household solution.

Children reaching grade 5 of primary school
Percentage of the children entering the first grade of primary school who eventually reach grade 5.

Crude death rate
Annual number of deaths per 1,000 population.

Crude birth rate
Annual number of births per 1,000 population.

Total fertility rate
The number of children that would be born per woman if she were to live to the end of her child-bearing years and bear children at each age in accordance with prevailing age-specific fertility rates.

Urban population
Percentage of population living in urban areas as defined according to the national definition used in the most recent population census.

Absolute poverty level
The income level below which a minimum nutritionally adequate diet plus essential non-food requirements is not affordable.

ODA
Official development assistance.

Debt service
The sum of interest payments and repayments of principal on external public and publicly guaranteed long-term debts.

Contraceptive prevalence
Percentage of married women aged 15-49 years currently using contraception.

Births attended
Percentage of births attended by physicians, nurses, midwives, trained primary health care workers or trained traditional birth attendants.

Maternal mortality rate
Annual number of deaths of women from pregnancy-related causes per 100,000 live births.

Main sources

Under-five and infant mortality
United Nations Population Division, UNICEF,
United Nations Statistical Division, World
Bank and US Bureau of the Census.

Total population
United Nations Population Division.

Births
United Nations Population Division, United
Nations Statistical Division and World Bank.

Under-five deaths
UNICEF.

GNP per capita
World Bank.

Life expectancy
United Nations Population Division.

Adult literacy
United Nations Educational, Scientific and
Cultural Organization (UNESCO).

**School enrolment and reaching
grade 5**
United Nations Educational, Scientific and
Cultural Organization (UNESCO).

Household income
World Bank.

Low birth weight
World Health Organization (WHO).

Breastfeeding
Demographic and Health Surveys
(Macro International), and World Health
Organization (WHO).

**Underweight, wasting
and stunting**
World Health Organization (WHO) and
Demographic and Health Surveys.

Goitre rate
World Health Organization (WHO).

Calorie intake
Food and Agricultural Organization of the
United Nations (FAO).

Household expenditure on food
World Bank.

**Access to safe drinking water and
adequate sanitation facilities**
World Health Organization (WHO) and UNICEF.

Access to health services
UNICEF.

Immunization
World Health Organization (WHO) and UNICEF.

ORT use
World Health Organization (WHO) and UNICEF.

Radio and television
United Nations Educational, Scientific and
Cultural Organization (UNESCO).

Child population
United Nations Population Division.

Crude death and birth rates
United Nations Population Division.

Fertility
United Nations Population Division.

Urban population
United Nations Population Division
and World Bank.

Inflation and absolute poverty level
World Bank.

**Expenditure on health, education
and defense**
International Monetary Fund (IMF).

ODA
Organisation for Economic Co-operation and
Development (OECD).

Debt service
World Bank.

Contraceptive prevalence
United Nations Population Division,
Rockefeller Foundation and Demographic
and Health Surveys.

Births attended
World Health Organization (WHO).

Maternal mortality
World Health Organization (WHO).

UNICEF Headquarters
3 UN Plaza
New York, NY 10017, USA

UNICEF Geneva Office
Palais des Nations
CH–1211 Geneva 10, Switzerland

UNICEF Regional Office for
Eastern and Southern Africa
P.O. Box 44145
Nairobi, Kenya

UNICEF Regional Office for
West and Central Africa
P.O. Box 443
Abidjan 04, Côte d'Ivoire

UNICEF Regional Office for the
Americas and the Caribbean
Apartado Aéreo 7555
Santa Fe de Bogotá, Colombia

UNICEF Regional Office for
East Asia and the Pacific
P.O. Box 2–154
Bangkok 10200, Thailand

UNICEF Regional Office for the
Middle East and North Africa
P.O. Box 811721
11181 Amman, Jordan

UNICEF Regional Office
for South Asia
P.O. Box 5815
Lekhnath Marg
Kathmandu, Nepal

UNICEF Office for Japan
UN Headquarters Building
8th floor
53–70, Jingumae 5–chome
Shibuya–ku
Tokyo 150, Japan